TWELVE-STEP GUIDE TO USING THE ALCOHOLICS ANONYMOUS BIG BOOK

TWELVE-STEP GUIDE TO USING THE ALCOHOLICS ANONYMOUS BIG BOOK

PERSONAL TRANSFORMATION:

The Promise of the Twelve-Step Process

Herb K.
Palos Verdes, CA

Twelve-Step Guide to Using the Alcoholics Anonymous *Big Book*;
Personal Transformation: *The* Promise of the Twelve-Step Process
Copyright 2001 by Herb K.

All rights reserved. No part of this book, other than Appendix 2 and Appendix 9, may be reproduced or transmitted in any manner whatsoever without written permission from the publisher. For information write Capizon Publishing, P.O. Box 3272, Torrance, CA 90510-3272, or email to publisher@capizon.com.

The brief excerpts from *Alcoholics Anonymous* and *The Twelve Steps and Twelve Traditions* are reprinted with permission of Alcoholics Anonymous World Services, Inc. (AAWS). Permission to reprint these excerpts does not mean AAWS has reviewed or approved the contents of this publication, or that AAWS necessarily agrees with the views expressed here. A.A. is a program of recovery from alcoholism only. The use of these excerpts in connection with programs and activities that are patterned after A.A. but that address other problems, or in any other non-A.A. context, does not imply otherwise.

Cover design by Miles T. and Carl M.

Publisher's Cataloging-in-Publication
K., Herb (1940 -   )
Twelve-Step Guide to Using the Alcoholics Anonymous *Big Book*;
Personal Transformation: *The* Promise of the Twelve-Step Process
__ p. __ cm.
   1. Twelve-step programs
Library of Congress Control Number 2004104359
ISBN13   978-0-9659672-2-8

Capizon Publishing   www.capizon.com
Printed in the USA
Sixth Printing   June 2018

A Chinese Legend

Look at that curve in the River of Ch'i
With the green bamboos so luxuriant.

The Book of Songs (Waley)

Once upon a time, in the heart of the Western Kingdom, lay a beautiful garden. And there in the cool of the day the Master of the Garden liked to walk. Of all the denizens of the garden, the most beautiful and most beloved was a gracious and noble bamboo. Year after year, Bamboo grew yet more noble and gracious, conscious of his Master's love and watchful delight, but modest and gentle. And often, when Wind came to revel in the garden, Bamboo would cast aside his grave stateliness, to dance and play right merrily, tossing and swaying and leaping and bowing in joyous abandon, leading the Great Dance of the Garden which most delighted the Master's heart.

Now upon a day, the Master himself drew near to contemplate his Bamboo with eyes of curious expectancy. And Bamboo, in a passion of adoration, bowed his great head to the ground in loving greeting. The Master spoke: "Bamboo, Bamboo, I would use thee."

Bamboo flung his head to the sky in utter delight. The day of days had come, the day for which he had been made, the day to which he had been growing hour by hour, the day in which he would find his completion and his destiny. His voice came low: "Master, I am ready. Use me as thou wilt."

"Bamboo"—the Master's voice was grave—"I would take thee and—cut thee down!"

A trembling of a great horror shook Bamboo. "Cut ... me ... down? Me ... whom thou, Master, hast made the most beautiful in all thy garden ... cut me down? Ah, not that, not that. Use me for thy joy, O Master, but cut me not down!"

"Beloved Bamboo"—the Master's voice grew graver still—"if I cut thee not down, I cannot use thee."

The garden grew still. Wind held his breath. Bamboo slowly bent his proud and glorious head. There came a whisper: "Master, if thou cannot use me without cutting me down, then ... do thy will and cut."

"Bamboo, beloved Bamboo, I would ... cut thy leaves and branches from thee also."

"Master, Master, spare me. Cut me down and lay my beauty in the dust; but must thou take from me my leaves and branches also?"

"Bamboo, alas, if I cut them not away, I cannot use thee."

The sun hid his face. A listening butterfly glided fearfully away. And Bamboo shivered in terrible expectancy, whispering low: "Master, cut away."

"Bamboo, Bamboo, I would ... cleave thee in two and cut out thine heart, for if I cut not so, I cannot use thee."

Then was Bamboo bowed to the ground. "Master, Master ... then cut and cleave."

So did the Master of the garden take Bamboo and cut him down and hack off his branches and strip off his leaves and cleave him in two and cut out his heart. And lifting him gently, the Master carried him to where was a spring of fresh, sparkling water in the midst of his dry fields. Then putting one end of broken Bamboo in the spring and the other end into the water channel in his field, the Master laid down gently his beloved Bamboo. And the spring sang welcome and the clear sparkling waters raced joyously down the channel of Bamboo's torn body into the waiting fields. Then the rice was planted, and the days went by, and the shoots grew and the harvest came.

In that day was Bamboo, once so glorious in his stately beauty, yet more glorious in his brokenness and humility. For in his beauty he was life abundant, but in his brokenness he became a channel of abundant life to his Master's world.

From *In the Shadow of Nine Dragons*, Eric Hague. London: Highway Press, 1958.

TABLE OF CONTENTS

Acknowledgments: We Are Community	ix
Preface: Purpose of This Guide	1
The Doctor's Opinion	3
Introduction: My Experience with the Recovery Process	5
Step Process: Assignment Focus and Intent	13
***Big Book* Contents: How It Is Organized**	15
Reflection	17
Preparation to Do This Work: How to Begin	
Assignment # 1	19
Step One . . . . Powerlessness	
Assignment # 2	23
Assignment # 3	25
Assignment # 4	27
Step Two . . . . Faith	
Assignment # 5	32
Step Three . . . . Decision	
Assignment # 6	38
Step Four . . . . Inventory	
Assignment # 7	44
Assignment # 8	48
Assignment # 9	51
Assignment # 10	53
Assignment # 11	56
Assignment # 12	60
Assignment # 13	63
Step Five . . . . Disclosure	
Assignment # 14	65

Step Six . . . . **Readiness**
    Assignment # 15   70

Step Seven . . . . **Prayer**
    Assignment # 16   74

Step Eight . . . . **Making a List**
    Assignment # 17   77

Step Nine . . . . **Making Amends**
    Assignment # 18   81

Step Ten . . . . **"Spot Check" Inventory**
    Assignment # 19   85

Step Eleven . . . . **Prayer and Meditation**
    Assignment # 20   89

Step Twelve . . . . **Carrying the Message;**
                                                            Practicing the Principles
    Assignment # 21   93

Final Reflection   97

Appendices: Helpful Tools
    1. The A.A. Symbol Analyzed   100
    2. Resentment Worksheet   101
    3. Outline of Step Ten   104
    4. Outline of Step Eleven   105
    5. Outline of Step Twelve   109
       (Summary of Instructions in *Big Book* Chapter 7)
    6. My Personal Morning Prayer and Meditation Practice   111
    7. My Personal Evening Prayer and Meditation Practice   114
    8. Principles   116
    9. Meeting Formats
        Big Book Step Study Meeting (A.A.)   120
        Big Book Text Study Meeting (A.A.)   123
        Big Book Step Workshop (Open)   124
        Big Book Step Study Meeting (Open)   127

Acknowledgments
We Are Community

This guide was made possible through the Grace of God, the support of hundreds of A.A. meetings, and the specific help of a number of recovered alcoholics. There are a few very special people without whom it would have been impossible:

Mary K.	My loyal wife, who, in 1984, introduced me to the circumstances in which the foundational question was asked.
Phil B.	The hospital counselor who asked the question: "What is your story, your relationship with alcohol?"
Lloyd A.	My sponsor and friend, who modeled the A.A. way of life and patiently listened to me for these many years.
Jerry R.	My first step guide (1988), who turned the light on the *Big Book* and made *it* my guide. The powerlessness connected to the *physical allergy* was revealed.
Rod S.	My next step guide (1991), who knew I hadn't seen the first step at depth and patiently brought me to hopelessness. The powerlessness connected to the *mental obsession* was experienced.
Joe H.	My next step guide (1994), who knew that my unseen agnosticism was blocking my spiritual progress. He taught me how to ask the veil-rending questions that revealed not only the *spiritual malady*, but also my doubt, my *practical* agnosticism.

Allen Berger, Ph.D.	Who double yoked with me to till my psyche-soil so that my soul could grow, who also carefully reviewed this entire manuscript and offered many helpful suggestions to make it more useful, and who authored The Doctor's Opinion in this guide.
Luke and his Trappist brothers	Whose hospitality at the Abbey of Gethsemane turned a week's retreat into a writing event, producing the first draft of the manuscript for this guide.
Thomas Merton	Whose writings, tapes, and spirit inspired and energized me to bring this guide from concept to paper while at the Abbey.
Katherine Mears	Whose patience, diligence, and ability to read my hieroglyphics produced the many versions of the manuscript that made this guide a reality.
Daughters of Mary and Joseph Retreat Center	The community that first carried the message to my wife and continues to support us as we carry the message to others.
House of Hope	The women's recovery center that provided my wife and me a place to be of service and a mechanism for Step Nine amends.

All proceeds from the sale of this guide go to the House of Hope Foundation in San Pedro, CA.

Preface

Purpose of This Guide

This guide is not a commentary on the Alcoholics Anonymous *Big Book* (Fourth Edition). The *Big Book* (B.B.) contains all directions necessary to recover from "a seemingly hopeless state of mind and body" (B.B. page xiii) for those of us who are interested and willing to do the suggested work.

Bill Wilson wrote a commentary on his experience with the steps, first published in 1952 in the Alcoholics Anonymous *Twelve Steps and Twelve Traditions*. There are few directions in that book, but it contains wonderfully supplemental thoughts on the twelve-step process and results.

This guide is intended to be used in conjunction with these books in working the Twelve Steps. It presents clarifying instructions for approaching and studying both books.

Specific Assignments That Guided Me Through All Twelve Steps

The following material confirms the specific instructions I received and followed for each step. They include:
- Prayer
- Reading
- Consideration/reflection
- Writing
- Discussion.

I received these instructions from my step guide (sponsor). This person was not only my guide, but my sounding board for questions and my mentor/confidant for each discussion.

This is not a do-it-yourself process. The formula has been and always will be "simple and personal ... one alcoholic talks with another alcoholic, sharing experience, strength, and hope" (B.B. page xxii).

Some of us have found it useful to supplement the books and this guide with a set of three CDs recorded at a step presentation made by the author, which can be obtained from Easy Does It Books & Gifts:

"A Day in the Steps" – Herb K. (January 12, 2002)
Easy Does It Books & Gifts
3517 East Broadway,
Long Beach, CA 90803
877-507-6237 (toll free)

> The CD set is $30.
> Add $3 for each set for shipping.
> California residents will be required to pay the applicable state sales tax.

You will also find it helpful to have:
- A three-ring binder (not a spiral notebook)
- Three different color markers
- Lots of three-hole paper
- A dictionary.

* * *

You stand at the turning point.

"Remember that we deal with alcohol—cunning, baffling, powerful! Without help it is too much for us. But there is One who has all power—that One is God. May you find Him now!" (B.B. pages 58-59)

The Doctor's Opinion

Throughout my career as a psychologist I have been interested in why and how people change. Do we change by claiming a repressed experience from our childhood or by changing irrational belief systems? Do we change by integrating the shadow of our persona or by learning healthier self-talk?

Interest in these and other questions about the process of change spawned from my own personal journey in recovery. Whenever I had the opportunity to select a topic for a term paper or research project in school, I chose to investigate the process of change. I read what many of the great minds in psychiatry, psychology, and philosophy had to say about this topic. I studied Freud, Pavlov, Perls, Rogers, Maslow, Horney, Jung, Fromm, Haley, Watzlawick, Satir, Kempler, amongst others, and found that all of them had profound insights into our plight and how we could overcome and grow from our various wounds and sufferings.

When I started to apply the understanding about change that grew from this research, I discovered something remarkable about the Twelve Steps of Alcoholics Anonymous: that they embody a remarkable integration of both spiritual and psychological principles of change. Bill Wilson and his peers synthesized spiritual and psychological principles into a very powerful twelve-step program which facilitates both recovery from alcoholism and profound personal transformation. There is no other program in human history with the success that A.A. has demonstrated in helping millions of people recover from the terrible disease of alcoholism.

What you are about to undertake in this twelve-step guide is an incredible challenge. Only about half of you who start this guide will complete it, maybe even less. Even in A.A., it is the road less traveled, as few have taken such a thorough and painstaking course in application of the steps. Those who have followed this path have found that the benefits far exceed the effort. I encourage you to give yourself this gift and honor your commitment to recovery—to go to any lengths. If you do, I am confident that you will change (or more accurately—will *be* changed!).

Be rigorous, honest, and tenacious in your efforts. You have suffered long enough!

Allen Berger, Ph.D.

Introduction

My Experience with the Recovery Process

"Having had a spiritual awakening as the result of these steps ..." (B.B. page 60). This is the *promise* confirmed in Step Twelve: having submitted to, taken the action required by, and been brought through the prior eleven steps, a spiritual awakening is guaranteed.

The *Big Book* is not self-explanatory—at least that is my experience. I am college educated, but the instructions for this spiritual process eluded me—and I wasn't conscious of my lack of a spiritual awakening, even at four years sober. I was clueless even to its necessity or its possibility.

At the general direction of my sponsor, I had worked the steps, on my own, reading the *Big Book* and doing the best I could, with very few specific directions. My first step was about drinking events; second and third steps—about my cradle Catholic God; fourth step—about behavior; fifth step—a script-reading and therapy-mode disclosure; sixth and seventh steps—short, but ineffective; eighth and ninth steps—about *sorry!*, very sorry indeed!; tenth and eleventh steps—about prayer, which I viewed from my previous religious exposure (versus experience); twelfth step—seemed mandatory and mundane drudgery, not an honor and privilege to be of service.

In anticipation of my fifth-year milestone, I was given the inspiration (breathed into from the Spirit) to:

1. Rework the steps; and
2. Ask a man (not my sponsor, since I'd already done that in my first year) to help guide me through this process (this second thought was even more important than the first).

I had no idea this would change my life from the inside out. It brought me into an ongoing transformation that provides the emotional stability and spiritual development I had been pursuing through religion, therapy, and a variety of self-help programs for 30 years!

This man, Jerry R., introduced me to a very structured method of approaching the *Big Book* based on:
- Prayer
- Reading
- Consideration/reflection
- Writing
- Discussion.

He pointed out that the *Big Book*:
- ... is "the basic text" (B.B. page xi) telling "the story of how many thousands of men and women have *recovered* from alcoholism" (B.B. face page)
- ... has as its main purpose "To show other alcoholics *precisely how we have recovered* ..." (B.B. page xiii)
- ... describes "... a plan of recovery ..." (B.B. page xxv)
- ... gets us to ask the question ... "What do I have to do?"; "It is the purpose of this book to answer such questions, specifically." (B.B. page 20).
- ... gives "clear-cut directions ... showing how we recovered" (B.B. page 29 referring to Chapters 5-11).

The *Big Book* is about *answering* the question "But where and how ... are we to find a Power greater than ourselves?" "Its main object is to enable you to find a Power ... which will solve your problem" (B.B. page 45)—that is, lack of power.

Could it be a coincidence that the architecture analogy of "building an arch through which we shall walk a free man at last" [B.B. page 75] permeates the book whose cover is blue, as in *blueprint*—a specific "plan of recovery" [B.B. page xxv]?

INTRODUCTION

Based on my previous effort (in my first year of sobriety) of working through the *Big Book*'s steps on my own, with no specific guidance, it's clear to me that the *Big Book* requires assistance. For me the directions in the *Big Book* were not self-evident. I needed a step guide—a person who himself had been led through the step process, who could share with me his instructions and experience.

My step guide gave me homework assignments, reducing the process into manageable projects, one for each step.

He asked me to:
- Pray each time I sat down to do any of the assignments
- Read with intention, highlighting words, phrases, and sentences that spoke to me
- Review this assignment with consideration and pick out the most meaningful thoughts
- Rewrite the highlighted passages in my own words
- Call and make an appointment to get together and discuss the assignment when finished; we shared our respective observations, questions, and experiences on each *Big Book* page for this specific reading assignment.

This process (Steps One through Nine) took ten months. While I had several important "Ah-hah!!"s, the two most significant were:

1. My body chemistry is different than normal people. When I ingest alcohol I cannot predict what will happen—but I can predict that periodically I will drink more than I intended. I have what looks like an allergy, which sets up a *physical craving* over which I have no control. I am totally powerless *once I take that first drink.*

2. I have a role and responsibility for the turmoil in my life (fourth column of resentment inventory). This discovery paralleled Columbus's observation that the world is round—

my whole perspective changed. I found my troubles "... are basically of my own making" (B.B. page 62).

These results were revealed to me a couple of months after finishing my amends. I became conscious that I was no longer in conflict with my family, my work colleagues, or myself. The tension I was so used to experiencing in my everyday interactions evaporated. I began to experience a sense of peace and a demeanor of happiness. Life had become sweet. The promises I hoped would manifest in my life were now a reality.

About three years later (1991) I was moved to do the work again with a new step guide. The method and instructions were similar to what I had done in 1988, but there were important and valuable differences. I experienced new awakenings, new insight in several of the steps, especially:

Step One: My mind is powerless to perceive the truth about alcohol—my mind is fundamentally flawed, defective. I experienced "no choice" at a previously unknown core level. I had experienced that "strange mental blank spot" (B.B. page 42). I needed to fully concede to my innermost self (B.B. page 30) that I had a *mental obsession* over which I was powerless—even to see the truth when it is presented.

Step Four: My troubles are of my own making arising out of a distorted sense of self-esteem (third column of resentment inventory); I lived in delusion, a lie, believing it to be the truth. I am not who I think I am.

The process this time took six months. My spiritual evolution continued; my spiritual awakening widened and deepened.

In anticipation of my tenth anniversary (1994), I was inspired to do the work again with a different step guide. Once again, the method and instructions were similar to 1988 and 1991, but not entirely the same. This time it was a very meditative process. I was instructed to approach each step from the vantage point of my experience and practice with Steps Ten and Eleven. Furthermore, I was asked to turn the statements in the *Big Book* into questions.

This method/process cracked open the meaning of the sentences by relating them to *my personal experiences.*

It took two years (there were major time lapses [balking] between columns in Step Four). Once again, I experienced new spiritual awakenings in several of the steps; the most meaningful were these:

1. A deeper insight into *unmanageability* as the core of the disease—the spiritual malady; my will is radically (at its root) flawed—it has a natural (innate) tendency to choose self over all else. (Is this the *origin* of "sin" ... choosing self over God??). I am powerless to choose other than my self without outside intervention.

2. I came to understand that I had done the work previously with preformed ideas (a prejudgment) about God—bringing to the work a closed mind built around the previous "cradle Catholic God." This prior knowledge and experience had prevented me from seeing the truth: I had a shadow corner of agnosticism (doubt) which was made clear to me when I looked at how I conducted my life (not how I thought, but how I walked—self-reliant). I was really a practical agnostic.

The questions asked in the presence of Grace and willingness have been the trip trigger to my recovery:
- "What is your relationship with alcohol?" (1984)

- "What happens when you put alcohol in your body?" (1988)
- "Have you ever decided to stop drinking and found you couldn't (or that you changed your mind!)?" (1991)
- "What areas of your life are unmanageable? How effective has been your decision making, your use of your will power?" (1993)
- "Do you have any doubts about God?" (1993)

It has been my experience that when, in an atmosphere of prayer, a thought-provoking question is asked and a thought-filled bit of information is presented, the result is new knowledge—not just at the intellectual level, but at the intuitive level. We become just a little bit more awake, a little bit more conscious. Our perceptions are shifted; our being is changed, ever so slightly, ever so subtly.

Transformation is our life's goal. But *we* cannot make it happen. We can only be open to the process, and make ourselves ready to receive this gift. We can be taken to a place of willingness (grace), but we must be willing to be taken (our cooperation). As I said previously, for me, the *Big Book* is not self-explanatory. I needed a lot of help over a prolonged time to understand both the depth of my disease and my responsibilities in recovery.

As a result of my experiences, I wrote this guide to lay out the aggregate of instructions I received in the hopes that it might help others to see the "... clear-cut directions ... showing how we recovered" (B.B. page 29). I could not find these instructions or follow them without specific guidance from one who had preceded me on the path. Having a guide was like wearing a coal miner's helmet with a light on it—my guide was able to switch on the light so that when I read the *Big Book* I could *see* the instructions and when I followed them *precisely,* I was led to the Truth.

Many men and women have journeyed the twelve-step path *precisely*. Find one and ask for help. Does this person have what you want? By their fruits (actions, lifestyle) you will know them.

It's a matter of your life! Death does not scare me, but the dying process from here to there does. A drinking alcoholic's life is filled with pain; a dry alcoholic's life is filled with insanity. But the recovery process the *Big Book* outlines promises a "... high road to a new freedom." (B.B. page xxi).

Many of us find it quite helpful to support and sustain our recovery through attendance at two types of meetings (refer to this guide's Appendix for formats), especially while doing this specific step work:

1. *Big Book* Step Study. A 20-minute speaker relates their instructions for doing the step, their struggles, experience, and results. Each person then shares experience on this specific step. This creates an atmosphere of camaraderie, reinforcement, support, and a little peer pressure to be consistent in making progress. The meeting holds us accountable for our effort. It is a cross-talk meeting where anybody can ask clarification questions of anybody who shares. It stays very focused!

2. *Big Book* Text Study. Each participant reads a paragraph or two from the *Big Book*, then shares experience with those paragraphs. This is also a cross-talk meeting and also stays very focused!

This twelve-step process of transformation is a path that leads to an effective relationship with an accessible, personal God. The *Big Book* says "... we are sure that our way of living has its advantages for all" (B.B. page xiii). This means those with addictions other than alcohol and even those without addictions—"normal" people looking for an improved spiritual life—can benefit from this process.

"We shall be with you in the Fellowship of the Spirit, and you will surely meet some of us as you trudge the Road of Happy Destiny.

May God bless you and keep you -- until then." (B.B. Page 164)

Step Process
Assignment Focus and Intent

Working from a frame of reference is really helpful. This guide's Table of Contents confirms where to find specific instructions. The following serves as a road map—confirming each assignment's focus and intent.

Step One .... Powerlessness
    Assignment # 2:   Physical Allergy: Defect of My BODY (no power of decision)
    Assignment # 3:   Intellect: Mental Obsession; Defect of My MIND (no power of decision)
    Assignment # 4:   Spirit: Spiritual Malady; Unmanageability; Defect of My WILL (no power of decision)

Step Two .... Faith
    Assignment # 5:   Belief: Making a Decision *About* God

Step Three .... Decision
    Assignment # 6:   Surrender: Making a Decision *For* God

Step Four .... Inventory
    Assignment # 7:   Resentments (fight): Columns One and Two
    Assignment # 8:   Resentments: Name How You Were Affected: Column Three
    Assignment # 9:   Resentments—Being Rid of Deep Resentments
    Assignment #10:   Resentments—What Is My Role, My Responsibility?: Column Four
    Assignment #11:   Fear (flight)
    Assignment #12:   Sex (merge)
    Assignment #13:   Overview of Inventory: Dishonesty/Secrets/Guilt/Shame

Step Five... Disclosure
    Assignment #14:   Full Revelation of Your Story—Removal Process Begins

Step Six... Readiness
    Assignment #15:   Willingness to Name Character Defects

Step Seven... Prayer
    Assignment #16:   Humility: Ask for Removal—Process Continues

Step Eight.. Making a List
    Assignment #17:   Harms

Step Nine... Making Amends
    Assignment #18:   Justice: Reparation

Step Ten.. "Spot Check" Inventory
    Assignment #19:   World of Spirit: Identify Spiritual Tool

Step Eleven.. Prayer and Meditation
    Assignment #20:   Develop a Daily Prayer Practice: Relationship = *Conscious* Contact; Source of Spiritual *Power*

Step Twelve .... Carrying the Message; Practicing the Principles
    Assignment #21:   Service Through Principles—Source of Spiritual *Growth*

Big Book Contents
How It Is Organized

Once again, in the spirit of a frame of reference, the following lays out the structure of the *Big Book:*

Chapter			Page	Step
P		PREFACE	xi	
R		FOREWORD TO THE FIRST EDITION	xiii	
O		FOREWORD TO THE SECOND EDITION	xv	
B		FOREWORD TO THE THIRD EDITION	xxii	
L		FOREWORD TO THE FOURTH EDITION	xxiii	
E		THE DOCTOR'S OPINION	xxv	
M	1	BILL'S STORY *	1	
	2	THERE IS A SOLUTION	17	
	3	MORE ABOUT ALCOHOLISM	30	Step 1
S	4	WE AGNOSTICS **	44	Step 2
O	5	HOW IT WORKS **	58	Steps 3 & 4
L	6	INTO ACTION	72	Step 5-11
U		**CARRY THE MESSAGE:**		
T	7	WORKING WITH OTHERS ALCOHOLICS	89	Step 12
I		**PRACTICE PRINCIPLES:**		
O	8	TO WIVES SPOUSE	104	Step 12
N	9	THE FAMILY AFTERWARD FAMILY	122	Step 12
	10	TO EMPLOYERS WORK	136	Step 12
	11	A VISION FOR YOU COMMUNITY	151	Step 12

Exceptions to this structure:

* Bill's story:
pages 1-8 describe the problem = his powerlessness (Step One);
pages 9-16 detail his recovery = the solution (Steps Two-Twelve).

** "Unmanageability," the second half of Step One (the spiritual malady), is described on pages 44 and 45, page 52 ("bedevilment" paragraph), and pages 60-62 ("we are extreme examples of self-will run riot").

    66 pages = 34% of text is on Step One
    45 pages = 25% of text is on Steps Two-Eleven
    <u>75</u> pages = 41% of text is on Step Twelve
    186 (22 pages of actual text contained in the Roman numerals)

Reflection

It's only in naming and accepting our brokenness

that we can be healed, can be redeemed.

It is in facing our shadows that we are transformed.

Asking ourselves the right question is more important

than prematurely being given the right answer.

It is the cutting edge of the right question

that rends the veil to TRUTH.

Herb K.

Preparation to Do This Work

How to Begin

ASSIGNMENT #1
Focus—Do I Really Want to Do This Work?

Each step, as contained in the *Big Book*, has four components:

1. It defines the PROBLEM.

2. It describes the PROCEDURE.

3. It contains a PRAYER.

4. It reveals many PROMISES.

This guide does not attempt to identify, elaborate, or even to summarize the PROBLEM or the PROMISES for each step; these can be readily found in the *Big Book*.

The primary purpose of this guide is to focus on the second component mentioned above, the PROCEDURE (instructions, directions).

All individuals are entitled to have their own experience as they journey this path, led by the Spirit.

Underneath each of the steps is personal *powerlessness*—we are powerless to see the *Truth;* we are powerless to take the *actions*. Therefore, for each step, prayers were constructed for my own use, based on the principles, words, and suggested prayers from various sections in the *Big Book*. The specific PRAYER for each step will be found toward the end of the instruction for each step, just before the reflection questions.

We all come to this place with our accumulated knowledge and experience (drinking, newly sober, or with long-time sobriety). Our knowledge and experiences have made us who we are today and have given us the lives we have today. To have something different (if we don't want what we have) or to have something better (if what we have is good but we want more—quality and/or quantity), we need *new* knowledge and experiences.

Dr. Carl Jung, speaking to Roland Hazard, suggested the solution for the alcoholic who is still suffering to be a "... vital spiritual experience..." (B.B. page 27). He explained this as a "rearrangement" where "Ideas, emotions, and attitudes, which were once the guiding forces of the lives of these men, are suddenly cast to one side, and a completely new set of conceptions and motives begin to dominate them" (B.B. page 27).

1. Therefore, my instructions begin by asking you to use the following "set aside" prayer:

    "God, please let me set aside everything that I think I know about myself, my disease, the Twelve Steps and You, God, for an open mind and a new experience with myself, my disease, the Twelve Steps and especially You, God!" (Substitute "brokenness" for disease if you are not an alcoholic.)

    The essence of this prayer is based on several suggestions found in the *Big Book* to "lay aside prejudice" (B.B. page 49). It was developed by some *Big Book* thumpers in the Denver recovery community.

PREPARATION TO DO THIS WORK

I was instructed to pray this prayer each morning when I first awaken, that is, roll out of bed onto my knees and pray. I was also to pray this prayer each time I sat down to do any step assignment. The last time through this work, I was asked to construct my own "set aside" prayer, included here:

Father, please fill me with Your Holy Spirit.

Open up my mind and heart. Allow me to set aside my old ideas about myself, my disease (or brokenness), my spiritual path, and You, Father.

Please allow me a new understanding and a new experience of myself, my marriage, my disease (or brokenness), my spiritual path, and especially You, Father.

Please help me to grow in understanding and effectiveness, to develop a clear vision of Your will for me and the courage to cooperate with Your Grace.

Please help me to see the Truth.

Pray that you be allowed to approach this work not only (or not even) with your head (an open mind) but especially with your heart (*open*) and with your soul (*open*), to *know* the Truth in the core of your being!

2. Next, review *Big Book* pages 58, 76, and 79 with respect to the phrase "... willing to go to any length ..." Write down each complete phrase found on those pages and identify what each says and how they are different.

3. Then, read from the title page of the *Big Book* through page 164; *consider*, but don't answer (at this time), these questions:

a. Why do you want to do this work?
b. Why ... at this time?
c. Are you really willing to go to any length?
d. In what areas in your life are you being dishonest with yourself and/or with others?

4. On page 59 of the *Big Book*, read each step slowly, reflecting on the "consideration" questions in 3. above.

5. Reread pages 9-16 (the description of Bill Wilson's recovery). Highlight anything that Bill thought, felt, or did that you are resistant to or unwilling to think, feel, or do.

6. Now answer the "consideration" questions (in 3. above); write out your answers—no less than a paragraph for each question, no more than a page.

7. Review the A.A. symbol (circle and triangle), Appendix 1, to identify the three parts of the problem:

- Body—"physical allergy" that leads to the "phenomenon of craving"
- Mind—"mental obsession" that leads to ineffectiveness of self-knowledge, the "strange mental blank spots" (B.B. page 42)
- Will—"spiritual malady" that leads to "unmanageability," self-will run riot. "Selfishness—self-centeredness!" (B.B. page 62)

... and three parts of the solution:

- Unity (Fellowship) supported by the Twelve Traditions
- Recovery precipitated by the Twelve Steps
- Service directed by the Twelve Concepts.

8. Meet with your step guide/sponsor to review your written assignments and to get the next assignment.

Step One

(first part of first half)

Powerless over alcohol when it is *in me*

ASSIGNMENT #2
Focus—Physical Allergy; Defect of My BODY

1. Each time you begin the work, pray to get centered. Modify your set aside prayer to focus on the subject of this assignment, for example:

    "Please help me to see the truth about my *craving*, once I start to drink."

2. Read the *Big Book* from title page up to the top of page 23 (except pages 9-16). When reading the portion of Bill's story, pages 1-8, ask yourself if you identify your experience with how Bill thought, felt, acted, or drank. Turn statements made by the *Big Book,* such as "... basic text ..." (B.B. page xi), into questions: Is this really a text book? Are you really an alcoholic? What, from your experience, makes it so? Don't answer right away—reflect on and consider each question. Highlight what speaks to you.

3. Listen to the CDs or tapes (see Preface, page 2 of this guide) if you have chosen to include them as part of the process (listen only to the portion relevant to this assignment).

4. Answer the statement at the top of *Big Book* page 23: Does your personal experience "... abundantly confirm this"? Identify three personal experiences with the phenomenon of craving—what happens once you ingest any alcohol at all? What is your specific experience ... with control, *once you start to drink*?

5. Reread The Doctor's Opinion and *Big Book* page 17 to the top of page 23. Does your personal experience "… abundantly confirm this"? Consider both sides of each question: "Maybe it does; maybe it doesn't?" WONDER ABOUT IT!

6. Consider your answer to the statement at the top of *Big Book* page 23. When you feel you've had a new experience with the "consideration" questions, you are ready to move on.

7. Meet with your step guide/sponsor to:
   a. Share with each other the highlights and the personal reactions, thoughts, and experiences on each page of the *Big Book* reading assignment.
   b. Review the written work you've done.
   c. Share your three personal experiences with the "phenomenon of craving."

Step One

(second part of first half)

Powerless over alcohol when it's *not in me*

ASSIGNMENT #3
Focus—Intellect; Mental Obsession; Defect of My MIND

1. Change focus of the set aside prayer ... truth about your *mental obsession*.

2. Do the same reading/consideration as in Assignment #2 with *Big Book* pages 23-43: "mental obsession." Continue to ask the questions—Are you really an alcoholic? What, from your own experience, makes it so? How do Jim's story and Fred's story differ? What is their point?

3. Listen to the relevant portion of the CDs or tapes if you have chosen to include them as part of the process.

4. Identify three personal experiences of the mental obsession (such as *changing your mind*) after having made a firm decision not to drink or not giving it any thought at all (experiencing those "strange mental blank spots" [B.B. page 42]).

   Does the term "outright mental defectives" (B.B. page xxvi) describe your condition? Have you really lost the power of choice? When you made a firm decision to stop drinking, had every reason to stop (judge, spouse, doctor, employer), and had stopped for a time (a day, a week, a month, a year)—did you stay stopped? Did you drink again? Did you give it much (any) thought just before you began to drink again?

5. Do a prayerful review of highlighted material.

6. Consider your personal experiences—does this description of *defective mind* apply to you and alcohol? How applicable is the "hot stove" (B.B. page 24) analogy?

7. Meet with your step guide/sponsor to:
   a. Share with each other the highlights and the personal reactions, thoughts, and experiences on each page of the *Big Book* reading assignment.
   b. Review the written work you've done.
   c. Share your three personal experiences with the "mental obsession."

Step One

(second half)

Powerless over my will to choose other than my self

ASSIGNMENT #4
Focus—Spirit: Spiritual Malady; Unmanageability; Defect of My WILL

1. Change focus of set aside prayer ... truth about unmanageability; ... spiritual malady.

2. Do reading assignment (highlight/consider) from the *Big Book*:

    a. pages 44, 45 (down to "... which will solve your problem.")
    b. page 52 (bedevilment paragraph—"We had to ask ...")
    c. page 60 (last paragraph) through 62 (first two paragraphs), and ...
    d. page 64 (last paragraph, lines 2-6).

    In assignment 2.d., above, do you see confirmation of a three-part problem addressed by a three-part solution? Review triangle again (Appendix 1).

    Reread bedevilment paragraph on *Big Book* page 52, *out loud*, making it current and applied to you. Example: "I am having trouble with personal relationships." Do it once more. How does it apply when you're drinking? How does it fit now that you're sober?

    Use dictionary to define "bedevilment."

3. Write a response to the question implied in the first sentence of the last paragraph on *Big Book* page 60, "Am I convinced that my

life run on self-will can hardly be a success?" Use the bedevilment paragraph (B.B. page 52) as a benchmark.

4. Read Step One in A.A.'s *Twelve Steps and Twelve Traditions* (to which I'll refer as the *Twelve and Twelve*), then highlight/consider.

5. Listen to the relevant portion of the CDs or tapes if you have chosen to include them as part of the process.

6. *Consider* each of the bedevilments from the paragraph on *Big Book* page 52. Write out an answer from your personal experiences to the following questions:
   a. How well do you do on your own power? How effective is your will power?
   b. If each of these areas was exactly the way you wanted them to be, would that be enough to keep you sober?
   c. With the Power and Grace of God that you have been given up to this point, how well do you do in each of these areas?

7. Do a prayerful review of *considerations* for this last part of Step One (items 6.a.-c. above) "... my life had become unmanageable."

8. Do a prayerful review of Step One, looking at all three parts (defective body, defective mind, and defective will).

9. *Wonder/consider!*
   a. What areas of your life are you living (acting), not thinking or believing, as if you have power?
   b. Can you surrender when your powerlessness becomes your reality?
   c. Do you believe in *Grace*—that is, in the middle of these considerations can you be moved past where you are?

10. Then write out answers to 9.a., b., and c. above.

11. Do a prayerful review of *Big Book* pages 44, 45, and 52, reflecting on your personal experience of "restless, irritable, and discontented" (B.B. page xxviii):
    a. Review questions from 6. above.
    b. Answer: can you straighten out your life on your own power?
    c. Consider external circumstances versus internal circumstances; it is the function of the *ego* (false self) to keep your focus outside of yourself (physical and emotional turmoil).

12. Meet with your step guide/sponsor to:
    a. Share the highlights and personal reactions, thoughts, and experiences you've both had on each page of the *Big Book* reading assignment.
    b. Review the written work you've done.
    c. Discuss, in depth, your current experiences of unmanageability, self-will run riot, and application of the bedevilments in your everyday life.

13. Realize the purpose of the first three step assignments (#2, #3, and #4) is to bring you to a place of experiencing:
    a. Deflation of your ego at depth
    b. Hopelessness
    c. Powerlessness
    d. A sense of personal and inevitable doom.

A conviction that your "... human resources ..." (yours and others) "... as marshaled by the *will* ... failed utterly" (B.B. page 45) ... so that "The delusion that we are like other people, or presently may be ..." (read: ever will be) "... has to be smashed" (B.B. page 30). "We learned that we had to fully concede to our innermost selves that we were alcoholics. *This is the first step in recovery*" (B.B. page 30, emphasis added).

Step One Prayer

... to experience *powerlessness*.

Please God, bring me into this process and give me a new experience of powerlessness and unmanageability, as well as of Your Power and Spirit.

Make it clear that I am fundamentally flawed in all areas: body, mind, and spirit. Also, please reveal that You are willing and will do for me what I can't do for myself. I want to surrender to You and this process. But I can't on my own power. You have taken me to a place of willingness and I have been given the willingness to be taken.

This is a gentle but definite process of awakenings and awarenesses. I am willing to be led by Your Spirit—to have Truth revealed about me and about You.

The requirement for this spiritual evolution is complete, unqualified *surrender* of my self to You. On my own power this cannot happen. My self cannot submit. There is a quiet, gentle place where my willingness and Your Grace meet. I am willing to surrender and pray that You take me to that place.

Step One Reflection Questions

After prayerful consideration, write out the answers to the following questions:

What is the biggest difficulty/problem in my life right now?

1. Am I really willing to go to any length to have this difficulty/problem resolved?

2. Where am I being dishonest:
    a. With others?
    b. With myself?

3. What do "powerless" and "unmanageable," with respect to this problem, really mean to me? How are they different?

Step Two

Faith

ASSIGNMENT #5
Focus—Belief: Making a Decision *About* God

1. Change focus of set aside prayer ... truth about your Higher Power.
2. Answer these questions in writing:
   a. What areas of your life are you living as if you don't need power other than your own?
   b. What areas of your life are you living as if you control the Power of God that you do have? Are you relying on yourself exclusively?
   c. Who is God? How do you currently define/describe your Higher Power? What qualities does your current Higher Power have? What do you really believe?

3. Read *Big Book* Chapter 4 "We Agnostics", Appendix II (pages 567-568), and pages 9-16, highlighting what speaks to you. Pick out the five most important concepts and write them out in your own words.

4. Using a different color highlighter, read *Big Book* Chapter 4 *again*, marking every word and statement that helps you identify where you disbelieve, feel resistance, or have some doubt or skepticism.

5. Listen to the relevant portion of the CDs or tapes if you have chosen to include them as part of the process.

6. Once you complete 1.- 4. above, review your Chapter 4 highlighted words and statements, in prayer, with regard to

Step Two, first consideration (B.B. page 47): "Do I now believe, or am I even willing to believe ...", that this Power can take me beyond where I am (past the here and now; past the experiences I've already had) with every area of my life? (See B.B. page 52, the "bedevilments" paragraph for specific areas.)
   a. *Consider*: What is your decision?
   b. *Write* about your doubt!

7. Review your work on Steps One and Two so far:
   a. Mechanical review:
      - Do you have doubt?
   b. Prayerful review:
      - Physical craving
      - Mental obsession
      - Spiritual malady (bedevilments on page 52)
      - Doubt and Step Two, first consideration—Belief (item 4. above)

8. Step Two, second consideration: "... we had to fearlessly face the proposition that either God is everything or else He is nothing. God either is, or He isn't." (B.B. page 53).

9. *Consider*: What is your choice to be? What is your decision?

10. Consider the question "..where and how were we to find this power?" (B.B. page 45)

11. Review the possible answers contained in the third and fourth paragraphs on *Big Book* page 55:

   a. How:
      - "...search fearlessly..
      - "...think honestly..."
      - "...search diligently...."

b. Where:
- "We found the Great Reality deep down within us. In the last analysis it is only there that He may be found."

12. What does the word "attitude" mean? (fourth paragraph, B.B. page 55.)

13. Read Step Two in the *Twelve and Twelve*.

14. Reread *Big Book* Chapter 4 (mechanical review) using a different color marker to identify *positive* statements. Mark every word or statement that might help you go from your new willingness to believe this Power can take you beyond where you are with every area of your life.

15. With this focus (God is everything or nothing), write out your answer: What qualities or attributes do you need God to have for you today? (See last paragraph, B.B. page 62.)

16. As a helpful guide, also write out answers to these questions:
    a. How well do you do on your own power?
    b. How well do you do with the Power you've been given?
    c. How do you try to control the Power of God?

17. In one sitting, do another mechanical review of *Big Book* Chapter 4, marking additional words or statements and praying: "Please help me to extract everything I can that will help me move from where I am ... to choosing ... to be taken from the bridge of reason to the shore of faith."
    a. Take time every morning and evening, and whenever you can in between, to make those considerations in prayer until you're ready to choose—"God either is, or He isn't. What is your choice?" (B.B. page 53).
    b. Write out your answer: What does this choice really mean to you at this time in light of the experiences you've had?

18. Review all notes in your three-ring binder. Write a one-page spontaneous response in connection with whatever flows out of you after prayerful review.
    a. Do a prayerful review from *Big Book*'s The Doctor's Opinion (page xxv) to the bottom of page 57. Pause and consider:
       - Craving (top of page 23)
       - Obsession (bottom of page 43)
       - Unmanageability (pages 44, 45, 52, 60-62)
       - ABCs (page 60).
    b. In prayer, review *Big Book* Chapter 4's two considerations:
       - Page 47 "... believe ..."
       - Page 53 "... everything ..."
    c. After review, write a spontaneous response to this:
       What does this choice really mean to you at this time in light of the experiences you've had?

19. Meet with your step guide/sponsor to:
    a. Share with each other your highlights and personal reactions, thoughts, and experiences on each page of the *Big Book* reading assignment.
    b. Review the written work you've done.
    c. Discuss your description of the qualities or attributes you *need* your Higher Power to have (from question 15. above).

Step Two Prayer

... to develop a concept *about* Higher Power ... *about* God.

> God, I truly do (or want to) believe that You are a Power greater than myself who can take me beyond where I am right now. You can give me a new experience with You, a new faith in You, a certainty that I've never had. To make a choice that You are indeed Everything means my priorities will be rearranged. I can trust You if I really sincerely and honestly ask You to direct my *thinking* and my *willing* (decision/action). I can trust You even when I'm not sincere and honest (it's *me* I can't trust).
>
> I am not capable of the kind of commitment that comes with this territory. It appears that I'm not willing to really let go and operate on inspiration. If You are Everything, then You are my priority and I will be anxious to listen in prayer and meditation in the morning to Your direction, and will frequently pause during the day to check myself in relation to this direction.
>
> If You are Everything, then all that is and all that happens is You. All I need to do is be in harmony with my surroundings (people, places, and things), be conscious of Your presence, and be open to Your Spirit (in-spiration). This means cooperating with Your nudgings.
>
> If you are Everything, then I will at night consistently review my day to open myself to Your discipline/Spirit.
>
> If You are Everything, then *what is* Your will and I will be grateful. If You are Everything, then I will live in awe of reality with respect for Everything!

Step Two Reflection Questions

After prayerful consideration, write out the answers to the following questions:

1. What is my current concept of my Higher Power? What qualities does my current Higher Power have?

2. What are my doubts about God's:
    a. Existence?
    b. Knowledge?
    c. Power?
    d. Love?
    e. Presence?
    f. Accessibility?

3. How do these doubts manifest in the way I think, feel, and act?

4. What qualities do I need my Higher Power to have?

5. Where is God?

Step Three

Decision

ASSIGNMENT #6
Focus—Surrender: Making a Decision *For* God

1. Change focus of set aside prayer ... truth about surrender.

2. Read *Big Book* pages 58-63, highlighting what speaks to you.

3. Listen to the relevant portion of the CDs or tapes if you have chosen to include them as part of the process.

4. In light of the Step Three requirement on *Big Book* page 60 concerning self-will (last paragraph), write a spontaneous response to this:

    What does this choice really mean to you at this time of your life, considering the experiences you've had with being convinced your life run on self-will can hardly be a success?

5. Review *Big Book* page 58.
    a. Paragraph 1—Does this paragraph describe you functioning on your own power?
    b. Paragraph 2—Reaffirm Assignment #1. From where you are now, consider the four questions presented earlier in this text:
        - Why do you want to do this work?
        - Why ... at this time?
        - Are you really willing to go to any length?
        - In what areas in your life are you being dishonest with yourself and/or with others?

STEP THREE

6. On *Big Book* page 59, read each step slowly, looking at these "consideration" questions and then writing out answers.

7. Supplement written response to the "Step Three requirement" in exercise 4. above: what does this choice really mean?

8. Consider paragraph before ABCs (B.B. page 60): What does it mean to you in light of your current experiences?

9. Review ABCs (B.B. page 60) in your own way (meditation?).

10. Read with consideration (as a set of questions) *Big Book* page 60 (last paragraph) to page 62 (not including last paragraph). Focus on whether you're convinced that your life run on self-will can hardly be a success.

11. Add any additional reflection to "... self-will ..." commentary in exercise 4. above.

12. *Consider separately* what each term means to you (down *and* across):

Me	God
Actor	Director
Agent	Principal
Child	Father
Employee	Employer
Creature	Maker/Creator

13. Write out a definition of each term in 12. above.

14. In light of the Step Three decision on *Big Book* page 62 ("Next, we decided ..."), write out a spontaneous response in reaction to this:
    Are you, from this new place, ready to decide that hereafter in this life you would like God to be your

39

Director, Principal, and Father and you would like to be His actor, agent, and child?

15. On *Big Book* page 63, *consider* the second and third paragraphs, especially:
    a. "We thought well ..."
    b. "... that we could at last abandon ourselves utterly ..."
    c. "... voicing it without reservation."

16. Know that these are *ideals*—we are actually powerless to achieve them, but must be willing to be taken there by the grace of the Higher Power we've begun to make contact with, through Step Two.

17. On *Big Book* page 63, first paragraph, write out a new response to each question:
    a. Can you do this on your own power?
    b. Consider the paragraph in light of the questions from Assignment #1:
       • Why do you want to do this work?;
       • Why ... at this time?
       • Are you really willing to go to any length?
       • In what areas in your life are you being dishonest with yourself and/or with others?
    c. What is your vision of what that decision might mean?

18. Read Step Three in the *Twelve and Twelve*.

19. Do a prayerful review of all written material in your notebook (in one sitting); write a spontaneous response at the end of your prayerful review.

20. In prayer, formally make the decision to turn your will and life over to the *care* of God.

STEP THREE

21. Construct a personal Third Step prayer based on principles of the prayer on *Big Book* page 63 (see example on next page).

22. Make an appointment with your step guide/sponsor to:
    a. Review your experiences with each page of the *Big Book* assignment.
    b. Read and discuss all written work.
    c. Sit quietly in meditation for a short period.
    d. Get on your knees and hold hands.
    e. Pray your personal Third Step prayer out loud.
    f. Together, pray the Third Step prayer from *Big Book* page 63.

23. Obtain the instructions for Step Four.

Step Three Prayer

... to surrender ... to make a decision *for* God.

>My Creator, You have given me life and an opportunity to enjoy Your Love. However, I am naturally flawed in body, mind, and spirit—I think and act only out of self-interest.
>
>I believe that You are all *Knowledge*, *Power*, and *Love*—that You are *Everything*! I believe that You dwell deep down inside of me and that You can redirect my thinking and actions.
>
>Without any reservations and with utter abandonment, I humbly ask You to free me from this bondage of self. I pray that You transform my thinking to be consciously in relation to You as (pick one): Director, Principal, Father, Employer, Creator. I wholeheartedly offer You my free will and ask You to move me to complete surrender so that I will be restored to a natural alignment with Your Spirit, and my only intention and motive will be "Thy will be done."
>
>Please allow my life to be a witness of Your Power and Love so that others may be attracted to You and place their lives in harmony with Yours.

Step Three Reflection Questions

After prayerful consideration, write out the answers to the following questions:

1. Am I really convinced that my life, run on self-will, can hardly be a success?

2. What relationship do I want with this Higher Power: child; agent; employee; actor; creature?

3. Am I willing to make a decision to turn my life (what I have) and my will (what I want) over to the *care* of God?

4. What would my life (my actions) look like if I really *abandoned myself utterly* to God and relied on God *without reservation*?

Step Four

Inventory

ASSIGNMENT #7
Focus—Resentments (fight): Columns One and Two

1. Change focus of set aside prayer ... truth about resentments.

2. Construct a prayer for resentment inventory—use concepts discussed on *Big Book* page 64 (see example at the end of this assignment). Use both prayers morning and evening, as well as whenever you sit down to write.

3. Read *Big Book* pages 63-67. Highlight whatever jumps out at you. Reread, list, and define all synonyms for resentment, such as anger, sore, etc.

4. Listen to the relevant portion of the CDs or tapes if you have chosen to include them as part of the process.

5. Read Step Four from the *Twelve and Twelve*.

6. Each time you sit down to write, get centered and review Steps One, Two, and Three in the *Big Book*, page 59.

7. Meet with your step guide/sponsor to:
   a. Share with each other your highlights and personal reactions, thoughts, and experiences on each page of the *Big Book* reading assignment.
   b. Review the written work you've done.

8. *Big Book* page 65 shows examples of setting up the resentment analysis in three columns. The following instructions detail how

to proceed. The instructions for Columns One and Two help you prepare a list that will then be used for the Column Three and Column Four analyses. A sample of the Column Three worksheet is at the end of this assignment. Worksheets for Column Three and Column Four that can be photocopied onto two-sided paper are in Appendix 2.

9. Column One: Begin listing your resentments (if you have done an inventory previously, list only those you still have—old or new). This will become the first column: "... people, institutions, and principles with whom we were angry" (B.B. page 64). Write a short prayer at the top of the page; for example, "God, please reveal my resentments."

   Allow names to flow out; trust what comes—think of each name as a *gift*; do not filter or judge it. Record your thoughts freely, without regard to order or neatness. Review your entire life in two phases:

   a. Spontaneous outpouring; stream of consciousness; memory dump (from head, heart, and gut).
   b. Organized review of life in buckets of time, for instance 0-5 years (preschool), 6-12 (preteen), and probably each year thereafter. Remember all the people and events in your life during these years: relatives, neighbors, playmates, boyfriends, girlfriends, teachers, coaches, priests/ministers/rabbis, friends, employers, colleagues, etc. List each name that creates a negative sensation, a heartburn, a tight tummy or clenched jaw.

   To generate ideas, consider the *bedevilments* paragraph on *Big Book* page 52, and the list of unresolved areas from your notebook. Check the list for repeats. Sit with it for a few days until you're sure there are no more. Keep it current for new resentments or new memories that emerge.

10. Column Two: To reveal the cause of your injuries ... what they did to you:

    a. From your completed Column One list, take the first name and put it on a piece of paper; number it; then let Column Two flow (use letters A, B, C for different resentments under each number [same name]). Here's an example:

        #1 Jack (a coworker):
            A.   Tried to get me fired
            B.   Was lazy and didn't do any productive work
            C.   Turned my best friend against me.

        List different resentments qualitatively (different actions/events) *not* quantitatively (the number of times of these actions/events). Be specific.

    b. For major resentments, allow stream of consciousness to flow on a separate piece of paper. Use this material to pick out Column Two items on each Column One person, institution, and principle. Keep your notes for use in Step Five.

Step Four Prayer (truth about resentments)

... to see the truth about *resentments*.

> God, please allow me to be thorough and honest in this inventory process—to discover the truth and find, then face, the facts, causes, and conditions of my failure.
>
> Please reveal to me my resentments and why I am angry.
>
> Please allow me to resolutely look for my mistakes—to see my role, admit my wrongs honestly, and be willing to set these matters straight.
>
> Please remove these things in me that are blocking me from the sunlight of Your Spirit.

ASSIGNMENT #8
Focus—Resentments: Name How You Were Affected: Column Three

1. Reread *Big Book* pages 64 and 65.

2. Listen to the relevant portion of the CDs or tapes if you have chosen to include them as part of the process.

3. Meet with your step guide/sponsor to:

   a. Share with each other your highlights and personal reactions, thoughts, and experiences on each page of the *Big Book* reading assignment.
   b. Review the written work you've done.

4. Prepare Column Three on why you were angry; something in you was "... hurt or threatened ... interfered with" (B.B. page 64).
   a. Begin Column Three using a separate worksheet page to write material for each letter item in Column Two. Write a prayer at the top of each page. If any resentments are repeats, combine them. Example:
   #1 Jack:
       A. He tried to get me fired.
   This hurt, threatened, or interfered with my:
   - Self-esteem
   - Pride
   - Ambition
   - Security
   - Personal relations
   - Sex relations (gender)
   - Pocketbook.

   > See worksheet on page 50 or in Appendix 2 for examples of how to analyze these.

   "Notice that the word fear is bracketed alongside the difficulties ..." (B.B. page 67). The worksheet in Appendix 2 is set up with a fear column to help you get insight into the true nature of the underlying "causes and conditions" (B.B. page 64) of this specific resentment. It will also help prepare you to identify your list of fears when you get to the fear inventory.

b. See the following worksheet for how to complete this "fact *finding* and fact *facing* process" (B.B. page 64, emphasis added). Make enough copies so you have one for each resentment, for example #1A, #1B, #1C, etc. (Refer to Appendix 2 for stand-alone worksheet.)

(NOTE: Place the Column Three worksheet on the left of your three-ring binder [punch holes on the right]. When reading for Step Five, this will put Column Four on the right side of the binder so you can read the third and fourth columns on the same resentment opposite each other.)

This is an effort to discover the *truth* about motives and values; "we searched out the flaws in our makeup which caused our failure" (B.B. page 64). What really was your underlying motive?

"Nothing counted but thoroughness and honesty" (B.B. page 65). This is a very revealing exercise. However, most of us initially find it difficult and require frequent meetings with our step guide to "break the code." The key to this analysis is being clear on *self-esteem*. All else flows from this concept. If you find this confusing (that is, the effort to define how self-esteem was affected), go to *pride*. When you define how you want others to see you, it will give you a clue as to how you see yourself.

Then go back to defining *self-esteem*. For example, if in *pride* you say you want others to see you as a superior person, then perhaps you really do believe you *are* a superior person.

This "self-esteem" is not who you want to be, or have been told you are. It is who you really *believe* you are.

Step Four, Column Three – Worksheet
 (see Appendix 2 for one that can be copied and used.)

Write personal prayer: "God, _____
_____"

Ask yourself: When I resented _____(Column One)
for _____ (Column Two),
did it hurt, threaten, or interfere with my:

What is my fear?
(May be the opposite of my belief)

Self-esteem: (my deep down belief about who I am)
I am _____
_____   [   ]

Pride: (how I want others to see me being treated by [Column One name])
Others should see (Column One name) _____ treating me as:
_____
_____   [   ]

Ambition: (what do I want?)
I want _____
_____   [   ]

Security: (what do I need? why do I need it?)
I need _____
_____   [   ]

Personal relations: (how should family, friends or colleagues see/or treat me?)
Family, friends or colleagues should always _____
_____   [   ]

Sex relations: (gender: what is my belief about men and women?)
The ideal/model man should always/…or is _____
_____   [   ]

The ideal/model woman should always/…or is _____
_____   [   ]

Pocketbook: (what is the affected value? For example: money, emotional security, etc.)
No one should do anything that interferes with, affects, or diminishes my
_____
_____   [   ]

Revised Dec 2008

STEP FOUR

ASSIGNMENT #9
Focus—Being Rid of Deep Resentments

1. When finished with all of your Column Three analysis, reread *Big Book* page 65, last paragraph, all of page 66, and through the first full paragraph (the first 13 lines) of *Big Book* page 67.

2. Listen to the relevant portion of the CDs or tapes if you have chosen to include them as part of the process.

3. "... consider it (Column Three) carefully" (B.B. page 65).

   Look for and mark with an X the "deep resentments" (B.B. page 66). Make a separate list of these deep resentment names.

4. "... turn back to the list ..." and "... look at it from an entirely different angle" (B.B. page 66). We must be rid of these for they "... shut ourselves off from the sunlight of the Spirit" (B.B. page 66). But we are *powerless* ... "we could not wish them away any more than alcohol" (B.B. page 66).

   Realize they are "... perhaps spiritually sick ... like ourselves ..." (B.B. pages 66 and 67); = the "... different angle" (B.B. page 66).

5. Construct a prayer from the material on *Big Book* page 67 to ask God to remove this resentment (see the next page for an example). Remember, the instructions in the *Big Book* don't say to pray for *them*; it says to ask God to remove this resentment from *you*.

Step Four Prayer (freedom from resentments)

...for removal of deep resentments.

God, (*name*), like me, is a spiritually sick person. Please help me to show (*name*) tolerance, compassion, and patience.

Please forgive me for being angry and enable me to stop clinging to this resentment. Please remove this resentment and show me how to take a kindly, and tolerant view of (*name*). Please show me how I can be helpful to (*name*).

Thy will be done!

* * *

> Pray your prayer for each person (seven deep resentments—seven individual prayers) each morning until you know in your innermost being that each resentment has been removed. Then cross that name off your list. Continue these prayers until all names have been removed. It was my experience that this took several months, but it worked—I have no remaining deep resentments.

ASSIGNMENT #10
Focus—What Is My Role, My Responsibility?: Column Four (or Final Phase of Resentment Inventory)

1. Reread *Big Book* page 67, first paragraph: "Referring to our list again ... we resolutely looked for our own mistakes."

2. Begin work on Column Four by looking at each name in Column Three and asking yourself "when I resented Column One name for Column Two cause , I had these beliefs about my role (Column Three "affects my")." Then, based on the instructions on *Big Book* page 67, write a response (use the second worksheet in Appendix 2; place it on the right side of your notebook):

   a. Define your role: What one or two words express your part in this drama—as if you were in a stage play?

   b. Is it true or false? ("... fancied or real ..." B.B. page 66—did the event actually happen or is it a figment of your imagination?) Add any more specifics in the margin, top right.

   c. Think about each resentment. Reflect on the questions and admit to yourself "... your own mistakes" (B.B. page 67). Write out a response to each of the following:

      - Selfish: Where were you thinking about yourself?
      - Self-seeking: Where were you acting on behalf of yourself?
      - Dishonest: In what ways did you misrepresent yourself?
        – By commission?
        – By omission?
      - Afraid: In what ways did you anticipate a loss to yourself, or not getting something you wanted for yourself?

3. For the four items above (Selfish, Self-seeking, Dishonest, Afraid), look around the entire event causing the resentment: before; during; after. Then answer:

a. Where were you wrong, at fault, or to blame (responsible)? What was your part in creating this situation or this feeling of resentment? What did or didn't you do (actual behavior)?

b. Is there any specific harm that hasn't already been included in the analysis of this resentment? Do not analyze harm; just list areas where harm to others may have been done:

- Physical?
- Mental?
- Financial?
- Emotional?
- Spiritual?

c. Write down any harm to each person (name them and the specific harm) other than the direct subject of this resentment. (This will help you in Step Eight—as suggested on B.B. page 76.)

d. Look through your Column Three and Column Four analysis and list additional fears (no explanation) at the very bottom. (Again, this is helpful preparation for the next part of the inventory assignment on fear.)

e. List any character defects that have been revealed to you in this analysis. Step Six is about being ready to have them removed—so it helps you name them. Also, naming them here helps you to get clear on the next item on the worksheet.

f. In light of the information coming from your answers on this worksheet, reflect on your *real* role (in contrast to the role you identified coming out of Column Three which is listed at the top of the Column Four worksheet). Your real role is usually the direct opposite of the perceived role coming out of Column Three. Column Three reflects our delusion, the "story", the lie; Column Four reveals the reality, the "facts", the truth.

ASSIGNMENT #11
Focus—Fear (flight)

1. Change focus of set aside prayer ... truth about fears.

2. Read and highlight *Big Book* pages 67 and 68.

3. Listen to the relevant portion of the CDs or tapes if you have chosen to include them as part of the process.

4. Meet with your step guide/sponsor to:
   a. Share with each other your highlights and personal reactions, thoughts, and experiences on each page of the *Big Book* reading assignment.
   b. Review the written work you've done.

5. Construct a prayer using concepts expressed on *Big Book* page 68 to have your fears revealed and removed (see example at the end of this assignment).

6. Center yourself in the presence of that Power you made contact with in Step Two, pray the prayer, and review Steps One, Two, and Three on *Big Book* page 59.

7. Identify fears from each completed resentment worksheet (both Columns Three and Four) and list them on a piece of paper (no repeats).

8. In prayer, ask God to let you see the fears you have that didn't make the resentment inventory. Review your entire life in two phases:
   a. Spontaneous outpouring; stream of consciousness; memory dump (from head, heart, and gut).
   b. Organized review of life in buckets of time. This is the same method you used to get your resentment list (see 9. on page 45 of this guide).

c. Add all fears uncovered by this process to the list.
d. Sit with this list of fears and look at their opposites; sit with your list in prayer until you know it's complete.

9. Take one specific fear from the list and number it.
   a. Describe the reason(s) you had this fear (what you're really afraid of). Ask "why is this so?" after each reason. Push it until you can't go any farther. Try to identify the *core* fear—the source of all your fears. Let it flow, for example:
      - Rejection   "I'm undesirable; no one will want me or love me; I'll be alone, in pain; I'll drink; I'll die; there is no afterlife; there is no God."

   Do this for each fear.

10. Look through each description to identify the essence or basic reason for the fear and distill down to the core fears where, for example, your list of 80 fears becomes a list of only 40 items. (Several may be synonyms for each other or were of the same family of fears.) Remember we are trying "…to get down to causes and conditions" (B.B. page 64).

11. Do the fear analysis process until you've reduced it to several core negative and positive issues such as:
    - dying / living
    - drinking / not drinking
    - failure / success
    - pain / pleasure
    - powerlessness / power
    - no God / God.

12. Identify your role (as in a stage play), like the resentment process for Column Four. "When I'm afraid of _____ because _____, and I have these beliefs about self-reliance, what do I (or don't I) do?" Write out a sentence or two about each fear.

Step Four Prayer (freedom from fear)

...to see and be free of *fear*.

>My Creator, please allow me to identify and honestly review my fears, to see underneath their symptoms to their root cause.
>
>Please allow my thinking to clearly reveal what You would have me *do* and then allow me to trust and humbly rely on You rather than my self.
>
>Please give me the courage to let You demonstrate through me what You can *do*.
>
>Please remove my fears and direct my attention to what You would have me *be*.

ASSIGNMENT #12
Focus—Sex (merge)

1. Change focus of set aside prayer ... truth about sex conduct.

2. Read and highlight *Big Book* pages 68-71.

3. Listen to the relevant portion of the CDs or tapes if you have chosen to include them as part of the process.

4. Construct a prayer based on the concepts on *Big Book* page 69 (see example at the end of this assignment).

5. Meet with your step guide/sponsor to:
   a. Share with each other your highlights and personal reactions, thoughts, and experiences on each page of the *Big Book* reading assignment.
   b. Review the written work you've done.

6. Make a list of sex events; trust what comes up and stay focused until you feel finished. Use the same process you used for resentment and fear (first a spontaneous memory dump, then a methodical review of your life). If you have done an inventory earlier in your recovery, only review events since then (or any that have not been addressed previously).

7. Take each name and place it at the top of a clean piece of paper and number it. Write a short prayer at the top of each page.
   a. In paragraph form, write a short history of that relationship:
      - Motive for getting involved
      - How the relationship started
      - Specific sex conduct
      - Major points that stand out
      - How the relationship ended, or where it is now.

b. Review this history and, for each name, answer the nine questions on *Big Book* page 69:
    - Where had you been selfish?
    - Where had you been dishonest?
    - Where had you been inconsiderate?
    - Whom had you hurt? (Look around the event—parents, children, spouse, etc.)
    - Did you unjustifiably arouse jealousy?
    - Did you unjustifiably arouse suspicion?
    - Did you unjustifiably arouse bitterness?
    - Where were you at fault?
    - What should you have done instead?

8. When done, use the accumulated answers to the last question ("What should you have done instead?") as a guide to develop your sex ideal (principles, values, standards). In prayer, ask God to mold your ideals and help you live up to them (B.B. page 69). Write out, in paragraph form, your chosen sex ideal as revealed *in meditation.*

This is not about *ideal sex*! It is about the principles, values, and standards you'll use as a basis for future conduct—your *sex ideal*.

Step Four Prayer (truth about sex)

... to see the truth about my *sex* conduct, to mold my sex ideal and help me live up to it.

> My Creator, You have given me sex powers and they are good. However, I have used them selfishly and dishonestly; I have been inconsiderate.
>
> Please allow me to see the truth about my selfishness—to see what relationships should be examined. Allow me to see where I was at fault and what I should have done instead.
>
> Please allow me to see where I have done harm and to be willing to make amends.
>
> Please give me healthy thinking about sex, mold my ideal, help me to be willing to grow toward that ideal and to have the strength to live up to it.

ASSIGNMENT #13
Focus—Overview of Inventory: Dishonesty/Secrets/Guilt/Shame

1. When you have completed all the previous inventory assignments, review to note all dishonesty and any new secrets that surfaced; also any actions, events, or attitudes about which you feel shame, guilt, or embarrassment.

2. Construct a prayer to become aware of the exact nature of harm.

3. Review:

    Resentment
    Fear   } Looking for additional instances and names
    Sex

    Add any current resentments, fears, sex events.

4. In prayer:
    a. Add to your sex ideal.
    b. Add any newly revealed dishonesty or secrets.

Step Four Reflection Questions (resentments, fear, and sex)

After prayerful consideration, write out the answers to the following questions:

1. What or who is my most irritating resentment?

2. Who am I in this resentment?
   a. Who do I think I am?
   b. ...believe I should be?
   c. ...want to be seen as?
   d. ...really believe I am?

3. Who am I really in this resentment? Where am I:
   a. Selfish: thinking about myself?
   b. Self-seeking: acting on my own behalf?
   c. Dishonest: misrepresenting myself?
   d. Fearful: concerned about not getting or losing?

4. What is my most bothersome fear?

5. Where is my selfishness/self-centeredness most prominent in my personal relationship(s)?

6. What is my sex ideal? How and why do I fall short of that ideal? Am I really willing to grow toward it?

7. Where am I being dishonest (by commission or omission) with myself or others?

8. What is the one "big secret" I have not been willing to *fully* reveal?

Step Five

Disclosure

ASSIGNMENT #14
Focus—Full Revelation of Your Story—Removal Process Begins

1. Change focus of set aside prayer ... to have the willingness to reveal the truth.

2. Read and highlight *Big Book* pages 72-75.

3. Read Step Five from the *Twelve and Twelve*.

4. Listen to the relevant portion of the CDs or tapes if you have chosen to include them as part of the process.

5. Construct a prayer about rigorous honesty based on directions in *Big Book* pages 72-75 (see example at the end of this assignment).

6. When ready, make an appointment with your step guide/sponsor to do Step Five.

7. Meet with your step guide/sponsor to:
   a. Share with each other your highlights and personal reactions, thoughts, and experiences on each page of the *Big Book* reading assignment up through page 75 second paragraph, first sentence, "... every dark cranny of the past."
   b. Review the written work you've done.
   c. Read your entire Step Four inventory to your step guide/sponsor
   d. After you finish reading Step Four inventory, return to *Big Book* page 75 and read aloud the entire second paragraph, emphasizing "withholding nothing."

Ask the question: are there any dishonesty, secrets, shame, guilt, or harmful actions that have not been discussed?
   e. Read aloud the promises (balance of second paragraph) and the last paragraph.

8. Once you complete Step Five:
   a. Go to a place where you can be quiet for an hour.
   b. Reread "Returning home ..." (B.B. page 75).
   c. Scan the inventory:
      - Have you withheld anything?
      - Are there any secrets not revealed?
   d. Review what you've done— *Big Book* page 59 first five proposals (steps):
      - Step One, *Big Book* page 17 elements in the cement (the **foundation**):
         – Common peril—powerlessness over alcohol
            = body: physical allergy; phenomenon of craving
            = mind: mental obsession
            = will: spiritual malady; unmanageability
         – Common solution—Unity (fellowship), Recovery, and Service (AA's triangle).
      - Step Two, *Big Book* pages 47 and 53 (the **cornerstone**):
         – Willingness and decision to believe—that God is and is Everything
            = decision *about* God.
      - Step Three, *Big Book* page 62 (the **keystone**):
         – Decision to surrender
            = decision *for* God
      - Step Four, *Big Book* pages 63-71 building blocks:
         – Naming the obstacles, impediments
            = *to* God:
               - Resentment
               - Fear
               - Sex
               - Dishonesty
               - Secrets

For we are building a "new and triumphant arch to freedom" (B.B. page 62), "through which we shall walk a free man (person) at last" (B.B. page 75).

Step Five Prayers

... to identify harm and become conscious of, and willing to reveal, all of my secrets.

>Father and Creator, please open up my mind, memory, and heart. Allow me to see and reveal the exact nature of the *harm* I have caused to each person directly or indirectly.
>
>Also allow me to see and reveal each and every hidden secret.

... to be rigorously honest.

>Father, help me to be honest with myself and the people in my life; reduce my egoism, fear, and pride. Teach me humility, fearlessness, and honesty. Help me have my outside match my inside. Make me willing to seek and take advice and accept direction. Please reduce my rationalizations and give me a true picture of myself and of the real world around me.

Step Five Reflection Questions

After prayerful consideration, write out the answers to the following questions:

1. Am I willing to reveal what I have written—totally; transparently?

2. Can I really be honest with someone; with myself?

3. Have I already made a decision to withhold something by not writing it down?

4. Is there any dark cranny in which I have not directed the light?

5. Am I willing to reveal all my dishonesty, secrets, shame, and guilt?

Step Six

Readiness

ASSIGNMENT #15
Focus—Willingness to See Character Defects

1. Change focus of set aside prayer ... to see the truth about character defects and become entirely ready to have them removed.

2. Read and highlight first paragraph on *Big Book* page 76 and Step Six in the *Twelve and Twelve*.

3. Listen to the relevant portion of the CDs or tapes if you have chosen to include them as part of the process.

4. Review your inventory (especially Column Four) to pick out and list your character defects. Distill them down to the core defects.

5. Sit in prayer (based on B.B. page 76—see example at the end of this assignment) with this list to determine your willingness/readiness to have each defect of character removed.

6. Consider:
    a. Are you ready to have your defects removed?
    b. *Can* God remove them all? (Does God really have your permission; does God really have the power?)
    c. *Will* God remove them all?
    d. Are you willing to have God remove (change):
        - Defects?
        - Motives?
        - Behaviors?
        - Beliefs?

- Attitudes?
- Values?

e. Are you really ready? Are you really willing?

7. Meet with your step guide/sponsor to:
   a. Share with each other your highlights and personal reactions, thoughts, and experiences on each page of the *Big Book* reading assignment.
   b. Review the written work you've done.

Step Six Prayer

... to be willing.

Father, I am entirely ready and willing to have You remove all of my character defects. Please open up my mind, help me raise my eyes toward the ideal character, and keep me ready and willing to walk in that direction.

Step Six Reflection Questions

After prayerful consideration, write out the answers to the following questions:

1. What is the most prominent obstacle I use to shut out the sunlight of the Spirit?

2. How is it manifested in thought/attitude? ... feeling/emotion? ... behavior/activity?

3. What is its source? What purpose does it serve? What is its value to me? Is it a compensation for a need or deficiency I perceive I have?

4. What do I fear might happen if I let go of this behavior?

5. How does this behavior protect me from pain?

6. What feeling does this behavior help me avoid?

7. Am I *really* ready and willing to have it removed? If not, am I willing to pray for the willingness?

Step Seven

Prayer

ASSIGNMENT #16
Focus—Humility: Ask for Removal—Process Continues

1. Read and highlight the second paragraph on *Big Book* page 76 and Chapter 7 in the *Twelve and Twelve*.

2. Listen to the relevant portion of the CDs or tapes if you have chosen to include them as part of the process.

3. Construct your own Seventh Step prayer based on the principles of the prayer in the second paragraph on *Big Book* page 76 (see next page).

4. Meet with your step guide/sponsor to:
   a. Share with each other your highlights and personal reactions, thoughts, and experiences on each page of the *Big Book* reading assignment.
   b. Review the written work you've done.

5. When you are ready, on your knees (subject to one's own religious practices), pray your own prayer or the Seventh Step prayer on *Big Book* page 76, *humbly* asking for the removal of defects. If a particular defect is troublesome and resistant, pray for its specific removal *daily* until it's removed.

   NOTE: Bill Wilson clarified there is no difference between "defects of character" and "shortcomings." He just didn't want to use the same word in consecutive steps.

6. Pray the Third Step and Seventh Step prayers each morning, as part of your developing prayer practice. (B.B. pages 63 and 76, respectively

Step Seven Prayer

... to have character defects removed.

> "My Creator, I am now willing that You should have all of me, good and bad. I pray that You now remove from me every single defect of character which stands in the way of my usefulness to You and my fellows. Grant me strength, as I go out from here, to do Your bidding. Amen" (B.B. page 76).

Step Seven Reflection Questions

After prayerful consideration, write out the answers to the following questions:

1. Am I willing to pray the defect removal prayer? Without reservation?

2. If I have a particularly stubborn character defect, am I willing to pray for its *specific* removal?

3. Meanwhile, am I willing to stop, or at least modify, the behavior—the outward manifestation of this character defect?

4. Am I willing to hold myself accountable, on a daily basis, to my sponsor/step guide?

5. Do I believe my Higher Power *can* remove this obstacle and restore sanity? Do I believe my Higher Power *will*?

Step Eight

Making a List

ASSIGNMENT #17
Focus—Harms

1. Change focus of set aside prayer ... to identify harm done and be "... willing to make amends ..." (B.B. page 76).

2. Read and highlight *Big Book* page 76, third paragraph: "Now we need more action ..."; also read and highlight Step Eight in the *Twelve and Twelve*.

3. Listen to the relevant portion of the CDs or tapes if you have chosen to include them as part of the process.

4. Construct a prayer based on willingness (see example at the end of this assignment).

5. Review the inventory (especially Column Four worksheet) and make a list of each person or institution (for example, employer) harmed. Examine the incident for any harm created to others.

6. Review your entire life history to identify people or institutions that were harmed but did not show up in your inventory. For example, people or institutions from which you stole—there may not have been any resentment, fear, or sex involved.

7. Prepare a 3 x 5 card on each person or institution (unless you have previously made satisfactory amends and no further action is warranted):
   a. Include name, address, phone number.
   b. Write out specific harm.

STEP EIGHT

    c. Write out, in prayer, your estimate of the appropriate amend.
    d. On the right side, indicate "willing" (+) or "unwilling" (-) to make amends.

8. Sort the cards according to the following four categories:
   a. Willing: Know where to find
                    Don't know where to find
   b. Unwilling: Know where to find
                    Don't know where to find

9. Meet with your step guide/sponsor to:
   a. Share with each other your highlights and personal reactions, thoughts, and experiences on each page of the *Big Book* reading assignment.
   b. Review the written work you've done and read each card to be clear on the following issues:
      - Actual harm done to the person or institution
      - Nature of the intended amend
      - How best to phrase your amend
      - The best way to make your amend (direct, indirect, or not at all).

Step Eight Prayer

... to be made aware of harm done.

> Father, please allow me to identify those I have harmed—to make an honest appraisal of the harm done and of the amend that is necessary. Father, give me the willingness to make these amends.

Step Eight Reflection Questions

After prayerful consideration, write out the answers to the following questions:

1. Have I made a list of all the people and institutions I have harmed? Is it complete?

2. If I haven't made the list, who and what in my life have been the most harmed (physically, financially, emotionally, intellectually, or spiritually) by my behavior or by my not taking action?

3. Am I clear on the harm and the necessary amend?

4. Am I willing to make the appropriate amends?

5. Have I discussed these harms and intended actions with my step guide/sponsor?

Step Nine

Making Amends

ASSIGNMENT #18
Focus—Justice; Reparation

1. Change focus of set aside prayer ... to change, to make reparation, and to become useful to others.

2. Read and highlight *Big Book* pages 76-84 and Step Nine in the *Twelve and Twelve*. Pay particular attention to "Remember it was agreed at the beginning (B.B. page 58—just prior to making the Step Three decision) we would go to any length:
   a. ... for victory over *alcohol*" (B.B. page 76, emphasis added)
   b. ... to find a *spiritual experience*" (B.B. page 79, emphasis added)

   Why do you think this admonition "to remember" is in Step Nine—*twice*?

3. Listen to the relevant portion of the CDs or tapes if you have chosen to include them as part of the process.

4. Construct a prayer based on the discussion on *Big Book* pages 76-84 (see example at the end of this assignment).

5. Use this approach:
   a. Make an appointment.
   b. Let the person harmed know why you are there: not only "...to put our lives in order" (B.B. page 77), but especially "... to repair the damage done in the past" (B.B. page 76).
   c. Tell them the harm—be specific.
   d. Then ask them:

- Do you want to tell me anything I did that caused harm I haven't addressed?
- Do you want to tell me how I hurt you, how my actions affected you?

Then listen.

e. Suggest to them how you intend to make reparation for the harm done.

f. Ask them: What else can I do to make this right?

Then listen.

g. Search for a mutually acceptable resolution; arrange the best deal you can (for all parties; not just yourself!).

6. When you have completed making amends to all the people and institutions you are consciously aware of harming (diminishing), increase the time of both your morning and evening prayers/meditations. In both sittings, ask to be shown any amends you're not aware of.

If any new transgressions are revealed, repeat the process, fill out 3 x 5 cards, review with your step guide/sponsor, and make the required amends.

When you intuitively know that you have completely finished your amends, give all inventories and lists in your possession to God in a way that's meaningful to you (for example, ceremoniously burn them, or unceremoniously dump them in the garbage).

Step Nine Prayer

... to make reparation; to change my life.

>Please give me a sincere desire to set right the wrongs I have done and let my life provide a demonstration of my good will.

>Allow me to put my life in order, but more especially, to fit myself to be of maximum service to You and the people about me.

>Please give me a helpful and forgiving spirit. Please give me strength and direction to do the right thing no matter what the personal consequences may be.

>My Creator, show me the way of patience, tolerance, kindliness, and Love.

Step Nine Reflection Questions

After prayerful consideration, write out the answers to the following questions:

1. Have I completed all the amends on my list?

2. If I do not have this list, am I willing to make reparation for the harm(s) identified in Step Eight's reflection questions? What do I need to do?

3. If I have not completed all my amends, am I *really* willing to finish this work? If not, what is stopping me?

4. What is the single most troublesome human relationship in my life? What am I doing, or not doing, to resolve it?

5. Am I willing to be held accountable, on a regular basis (daily/weekly), for completing these amends?

Step Ten

"Spot Check" Inventory

ASSIGNMENT #19
Focus—World of Spirit: Identify Spiritual Tool

1. You begin practicing Step Ten at the same time you begin making amends. "We vigorously commenced this way of living as we cleaned up the past" (B.B. page 84).

2. Read and highlight:
   a. *Big Book* pages 84 and 85.
   b. Step Ten in the *Twelve and Twelve*.

3. Listen to the relevant portion of the CDs or tapes if you have chosen to include them as part of the process.

4. Outline *Big Book* pages 84 and 85 (see sample in Appendix 3).

5. Construct a prayer from the material on *Big Book* pages 84 and 85 (see example at the end of this assignment).

6. Meet with your step guide/sponsor to:
   a. Share with each other your highlights and personal reactions, thoughts, and experiences on each page of the *Big Book* reading assignment.
   b. Review the written work you've done.

7. For however many days it takes, as part of your daily meditation, begin to look at each area of your life (B.B. page 52: money/finance, relationship/marriage, work, children, spiritual life, recreation, etc.). Write out *your vision* of God's will in all your activities (at least one paragraph on each component).

8. When you are satisfied with your vision statement, read and extract from it a *general intent* for your life and put the written material away. Do this in meditation.

9. When you're clear on this general intent, spend as many days as you feel you need (done as a meditation) to begin grounding or anchoring intent until you feel satisfied.

Step Ten Prayer

... that I may truly enter the world of the Spirit.

> Father, please ...
> - Help me grow in understanding and effectiveness
> - Make me conscious of my nature and behavior
> - Give me strength, inspiration and direction
> - Give me a reprieve today through maintenance of my spiritual condition
> - Allow me today to carry my vision of Your will in all my activities
> - Show me how I can best serve You—Your will be done!
> - Allow me to think these thoughts constantly; to use my will this way!

Step Ten Reflection Questions

After prayerful consideration, write out the answers to the following questions:

1. What does it mean for me to "enter the world of the Spirit"? Where have I been?

2. What is my vision of God's will for me:
   a. Spiritual?
   b. Physical?
   c. Emotional?
   d. Intellectual?
   e. Financial?
   f. Relationship(s)?
   g. Work?
   h. Community?

3. When I'm disturbed, do I reflect on the source of the trouble within me?

4. When I realize that I've been resentful, dishonest, fearful, or selfish, do I:
   a. Ask God *at once* to remove it?
   b. Tell someone *immediately* about it?
   c. Make amends *quickly* if appropriate?
   d. *Resolutely* turn my thoughts to helping someone else?

Step Eleven

Prayer and Meditation

ASSIGNMENT #20
Focus—Develop a Daily Practice:
Relationship = *Conscious* Contact; Source of Spiritual *Power*

1. Read and highlight *Big Book* pages 85-88.

2. Read and highlight Step Eleven from the *Twelve and Twelve*.

3. Listen to the relevant portion of the CDs or tapes if you have chosen to include them as part of the process.

4. Outline the instructions on *Big Book* pages 85-88 (see example in Appendix 4):
   a. "When we retire ..."
   b. "On awakening ..."
   c. "As we go through the day ..."

5. Construct a prayer from the material on *Big Book* pages 85-88 (see examples in Appendices 6 and 7).

6. Meet with your step guide/sponsor to:
   a. Share with each other your highlights and personal reactions, thoughts, and experiences on each page of the *Big Book* reading assignment.
   b. Review the written work you've done.

7. Develop your own prayer practice (see samples in Appendices 6 and 7).

STEP ELEVEN

8. Sit daily for a minimum of five minutes of prayer and meditation in the morning and five minutes of prayer and meditation at night. Gradually extend *each* sitting to 20 minutes or more.

9. Go on a weekend retreat occasionally (Bill Wilson's recommendation, *Twelve and Twelve*, page 89). Many attend at least one retreat a year.

Step Eleven Prayer

... to receive Knowledge and Power.

Use the prayer you constructed from information in the *Big Book* pages 85 to 88.

For examples, refer to:
- Appendix 6—Morning prayer and meditation practice
- Appendix 7—Evening prayer and meditation practice.

There is also the St. Francis Prayer:

"Lord, make me a channel of thy peace;
That where there is hatred, I may bring love;
That where there is wrong, I may bring the spirit of forgiveness;
That where there is discord, I may bring harmony;
That where there is error, I may bring truth;
That where there is doubt, I may bring faith;
That where there is despair, I may bring hope;
That where there are shadows, I may bring light;
That where there is sadness, I may bring joy.
Lord, grant that I may seek rather to comfort than to be comforted;
To understand, than to be understood;
To love, than to be loved.
For it is by self-forgetting that one finds;
It is by forgiving that one is forgiven;
It is by dying that one awakens to eternal life.
Amen."

Step Eleven Reflection Questions

After prayerful consideration, write out the answers to the following questions:

1. Have I established a conscious contact with God? Do I really want one? Do I believe it is even possible for me?

2. Am I committed to improving my conscious contact with God?

3. Have I developed my own daily prayer practice?

4. Each day, how much time do I consistently dedicate to prayer and meditation:
   a. Morning?
   b. Evening?
   c. During the day?

5. Do I believe prayer and meditation are as vital to the health of my spiritual life as air and breathing are to my physical life?

Step Twelve

Carrying the Message; Practicing the Principles

ASSIGNMENT #21

Focus— Service Through Principles—Source of Spiritual *Growth*

1. Read and highlight *Big Book* Chapter 7.

2. Read and highlight Step Twelve from the *Twelve and Twelve*.

3. Listen to the relevant portion of the CDs or tapes if you have chosen to include them as part of the process.

4. Reread and list the instructions for working with others, *Big Book* Chapter 7 (see example in Appendix 5).

5. Construct a prayer from the material in Chapter 7 (see example at the end of this assignment).

6. Meet with your step guide/sponsor to:
    a. Share with each other your highlights and personal reactions, thoughts, and experiences on each page of the *Big Book* reading assignment.
    b. Review the written work you've done.

7. Read and highlight *Big Book* Chapters 8 through 11.

8. After highlighting each chapter (8 through 11), meet with your step guide/sponsor to:
    a. Share with each other your highlights and personal reactions, thoughts, and experiences on each page of the *Big Book* reading assignment.
    b. Review the written work you've done.

9. Define what the *Big Book* means about "principles" to be practiced in all affairs (see Appendix 8).

10. You may want to attend or start a meeting focused on the *Big Book* to effectively carry the message that you've had a spiritual awakening, a personal transformation, directly as *the* result of these steps, as *precisely* outlined in the *Big Book*.

    Appendix 9 contains four kinds of meeting formats:

    - Step Study (A.A.—closed)

    - Text Study (A.A.—closed)

    - Step Workshop: how to take a group through the same *Big Book* step process you experienced (open to all who are interested in a spiritual awakening)

    - Step Study: to support participants in the step workshop, especially non-alcoholics who might not otherwise have a *Big Book* step meeting (open to all who are interested in Twelve-Step spirituality).

Step Twelve Prayer

... to carry the message; to be useful.

> Please grant me a real tolerance of other people's shortcomings and viewpoints and a respect for their opinions—an attitude that will make me more useful to others. Please allow me to constantly think of others, and how I may help meet their needs.
>
> Please help me perfect and enlarge my spiritual life through work and self-sacrifice for others.
>
> Please help me develop a sense of being in partnership and brotherhood with all those around me.
>
> Please make me an effective channel of Your life-giving Grace to those who are still sick. Let me witness that a spiritual awakening and a new freedom are available as the result of doing this work which leads to You.

Step Twelve Reflection Questions

After prayerful consideration, write out the answers to the following questions:

1. Do I really believe/have I fully experienced that the root source of all my trouble is selfishness/self-centeredness?

2. Am I convinced that the solution to my self-centeredness is *OTHER/other*-centeredness?

3. Do I feel resistance to basing my life on the principle of service to others?

4. In what ways am I *actually* of service to others now?

5. What are the principles I need to practice in my daily life?
    a. With my spouse/significant relationship?
    b. In my family?
    c. In my work?
    d. In my community?

Final Reflection

"We are in the world to play the role He has assigned" (B.B. page 68). *What is your role?*

Our Job

"Your job now is to be at the place where you may be of maximum helpfulness to others ..." (B.B. page 102).

The natural way for God to manifest and work in this world is through people, through us.

We have intellect and will, which lead to knowledge and action. The proper use of the intellect is to seek *knowledge* of God's will. Ask yourself: *what is my vision of God's will for me?* When we use our will properly, we align our will with God's will. Therefore, our prayer is *"Thy will be done."*

When we are in *harmony* with Creative Intelligence, the Spirit of the Universe which underlies all, our Higher Power is revealed to us and through us to others. We are possessed with a new sense of power and direction (B.B. page 46).

Therefore, because our job is to seek *knowledge* of His will and the *power* to carry it out, we:
- "... grow in understanding ..." (B.B. page 84)—*knowledge*.
- "... grow in ... effectiveness ..."(B.B. page 84)—*power*.
- ... stay in *action* and *service*.
- "... perfect and enlarge (our) spiritual life through work and self-sacrifice for others ..." (B.B. pages 14 and 15).

Here is the *Big Book*'s simplified formula:

1. Clean house—Step Ten   Remove obstacles (as they appear) to conscious contact with God deep down within ourselves.

2. Trust God—Step Eleven   Improve our conscious contact with the Source of Power.

3. Help others—Step Twelve   Live or fulfill our purpose; our mission.

Periodically many will go through the entire process again with a *different* sponsor or step guide. Some do it annually. Bill Wilson recommended "... annual or semiannual housecleanings" (page 89, *Twelve and Twelve*). My rhythm is about every three years. In prayer, be led by the Spirit to find your own rhythm and step guide.

* * *

"We shall be with you in the Fellowship of the Spirit..." (B.B. page 164) and someday perhaps we'll meet as we "... trudge the Road of Happy Destiny" (B.B. page 164).

* * *

Meanwhile, let us all "... live in thankful contemplation of Him who presides over us all" (Tradition Twelve, long form, B.B. page 566).

Appendix 1
The A.A. Symbol Analyzed

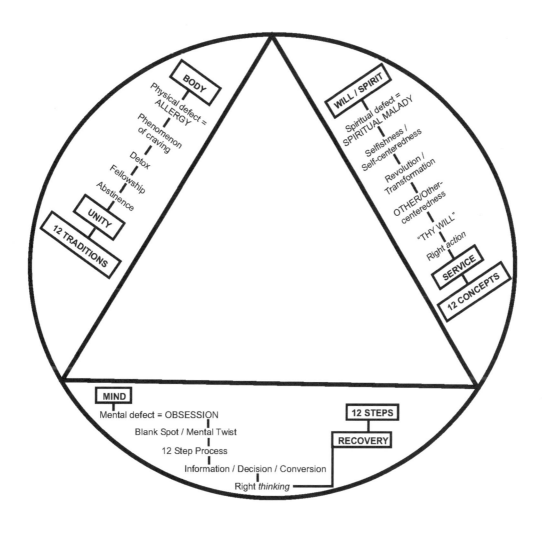

Appendix 2
Resentment Worksheet

On the following two pages is a worksheet for Step Four's Columns Three and Four, respectively. These may be photocopied onto two-sided paper, for as many copies as needed for your inventory. This makes Step Five more organized and easier to read because the third and fourth columns on each resentment page are opposite each other in your three-ring binder.

APPENDIX 2

Resentment Worksheet: Step Four, Column Three

Write personal prayer: "God, _____
_____ "

Ask yourself: When I resented _____(Column One)
for _____ (Column Two),
did it hurt, threaten, or interfere with my:

What is my fear?
(May be the opposite of my belief)

Self-esteem: (my deep down belief about who I am)
I am _____
_____ [   ]

Pride: (how I want others to see me being treated by [Column One name])
Others should see (Column One name) _____ treating me as:
_____
_____ [   ]

Ambition: (what do I want?)
I want _____
_____ [   ]

Security: (what do I need? why do I need it?)
I need _____
_____ [   ]

Personal relations: (how should family, friends or colleagues see/or treat me?)
Family, friends or colleagues should always _____
_____ [   ]

Sex relations: (gender: what is my belief about men and women?)
The ideal/model man should always/...or is _____
_____ [   ]

The ideal/model woman should always/...or is _____
_____ [   ]

Pocketbook: (what is the affected value? For example: money, emotional security, etc.)
No one should do anything that interferes with, affects, or diminishes
my _____
_____ [   ]

Revised Dec 2008

Resentment Worksheet: Step Four, Column Four

Write personal prayer: "God, _____
_____ "

When I resented _____(Column One) for _____
(Column Two), I had this belief about my role in Column Three:

My role:(like an actor in a play, for example: superior person, betrayed spouse, lovable child, etc.)
_____

Is the event true or false? (did it really happen?)_____

Consider before, during, and after the resentment and write one sentence answering the question:

WHERE WAS I...(at the time of the actual event), or **WHERE AM I...** (at present time)

1. **Selfish?** (*thinking* about myself) _____
2. **Self-seeking?** (*acting* on my own behalf)_____
3. **Dishonest?** (misrepresenting myself; lying by commission or omission) _____
4. **Afraid?** (fear of not getting what I want; or losing what I have) _____
5. **Where am I wrong/at fault/to blame** (responsible)?; Then and/or now?
   _____

6. **What harm did I cause to this person?** (how did I diminish this person?)
   a. Physical (body): _____
   b. Mental (mind): _____
   c. Emotional (feelings): _____
   d. Spiritual (relation with God): _____
   e. Financial (money): _____

7. What **harm** did I cause to *other* people, in and around this relationship? (write name and specific harm):
   _____

8. List any other **fears** you have become aware of:
   _____ _____ _____ _____ _____

List my character defect(s) _____ _____ _____ _____

My real role (now, in light of the Column Four information – usually the opposite of **my role** at top):_____

NOTE: 3 hole punch left side, or copy on back of Column Three worksheet   *Revised Dec. 2008*

Appendix 3

Outline of Step Ten

"We have entered the world of the Spirit" (B.B. page 84).

1. Essence of character building and good living

2. Process of emotional sobriety:
   a. Identify
   b. Admit/accept
   c. Correct

3. Formula:

   a.
Continue to watch for:	Use:	Produces harmony with others:
Selfishness	Self-restraint	Courtesy
Dishonesty	Honest self-appraisal	Justice
Resentment	Forgiveness	Kindness
Fear	Trust	Love

   b. Ask God *at once* to remove (the specific character defects).
   c. Discuss them with someone *immediately*.
   d. If harm done, make amends *quickly*.
   e. *Resolutely* turn your thoughts to helping someone else.

4. Our Code = Love and Tolerance
   a. Others are sick too!
   b. We cease fighting anything or anyone.

Appendix 4

Outline of Step Eleven

Preparation for Prayer and Meditation

Attitude: *prayerful attention*.

Purpose:

1. To improve my conscious contact with God.

2. To enhance my usefulness to others.

3. To develop humility, making it possible to receive God's help.

As you understand Him, God:

4. Is…
   a. Everything.
   b. Knowledge.
   c. Power.
   d. Love.
   e. Presence.

5. Resides…
   a. Deep down within me.

APPENDIX 4

In the Evening: Identify and pray for removal of obstacles to the sunlight of the Spirit.

1. *Constructively* review my day (without fear or favor)
   a. Was I: What motives were underneath my:

   - Resentful?
   - Selfish?
   - Dishonest?
   - Afraid?

   - Intentions?
   - Thoughts?
   - Acts?
   - Efforts?

   b. Do I owe an apology?
   c. Have I kept something to myself that should be discussed with another person at once?
   d. Was I kind and loving toward all?
   e. What could I have done better?
   f. Was I thinking of myself most of the time?
   g. Or was I thinking of what I could do for others, of what I could pack into the stream of life?

2. Ask God's forgiveness.

3. Ask what corrective measures should be taken.

4. Thank Him for blessings received.

5. Be willing to try again tomorrow!

Upon Awakening: Seek to *improve* my conscious contact.

1. Father, please direct my thinking, especially divorce it from motives of:
    a. Selfishness
    b. Self-seeking
    c. Self-pity
    d. Resentment
    e. Fear
    f. Dishonesty

2. Please clear my thinking of wrong motives.

3. *Think* about the 24 hours ahead (DO-ing).

4. *Consider* my plans for the day (BE-ing).

5. Please clarify my vision of Your will for me today (intent). How can I best serve You?

6. If I feel indecision: ask God to give me an inspiration, an intuitive thought, or a decision. Ask God to help me relax and take it easy ... to stop struggling.

7. Ask God to:
    a. Show me all through the day what my next step is to be. — Knowledge
    b. Give me whatever I need to take care of tasks and problems. — Power
    c. Especially free me from self-will. — Freedom
    d. Show me the way of patience, tolerance, kindliness, and Love. — Love
    e. Allow today's work to provide an opportunity for me to be useful and helpful. What can I do today for the person who is still sick? — Service

APPENDIX 4

All Day: Pray for *knowledge* and *power*.

1. Pause frequently when agitated or doubtful; ask for the right:
    a. Thought or
    b. Action.
2. Many times humbly say, "Thy will be done."
3. *Think* what I can *do* for others!

Appendix 5

Outline of Step Twelve

(Summary of Instructions in *Big Book* Chapter 7)

1. Find a person (drinker) who wants to recover (search out).

2. Find out all you can about them (to put yourself in their place):
   a. Indirectly, from a person close to them (their family).
   b. Directly from the problem drinker. Share yourself with them, especially attempt identification with drinking experiences).

3. Ask them if they want to quit for good and are ready to go to any extreme to do so.

4. Stress the hopelessness. Relate your specific experience with the physical allergy and the mental obsession. Help this person connect their experience to powerlessness with alcohol. Let them draw their own conclusion.

5. Tell them exactly what happened to you; stress the spiritual. They need to be willing to believe in a Power greater than themselves and to live by spiritual principles (but no specific dogma).

6. Be sane and quiet and full of human understanding.

7. Outline the program of action:
   a. Inventory
   b. Amends
   c. Daily prayer and meditation
   d. Service to others.

8. Tell them about the Fellowship. Tell them that if they want to get well you will do anything to help.

APPENDIX 5

9. If they are sincerely interested, give them the *Big Book* and ask them to read it.

10. Share your practical experience with the Twelve Steps. Make yourself available for the Third and Fifth Steps (and Seventh if requested).

11. Help them get a job, give them a little financial assistance, or provide shelter in your home. Help but do not enable. Recovery is not dependent upon people. It is dependent upon the person's relationship with God.

12. "Your job now is to be at the place where you may be of maximum helpfulness to others" (B.B. page 102).

Appendix 6

My Personal Morning Prayer and Meditation Practice

Prayer (on my knees)
1. Set Aside Prayer.
    God, please let me set aside everything that I think I know about myself, my disease (brokenness), the Twelve Steps and You, God, for an open mind and a new experience with myself, my disease (brokenness), the Twelve Steps and especially You, God!
2. Third Step Prayer.
    "God, I offer myself to Thee—to build with me and to do with me as Thou wilt. Relieve me of the bondage of self, that I may better do Thy will. Take away my difficulties, that victory over them may bear witness to those I would help of Thy Power, Thy Love, and Thy Way of life. May I do Thy will always!" (B.B. page 63)

Preparing to Meditate
3. Is my attitude one of prayerful attention?
4. What is my purpose?
    a. To improve my conscious contact with God.
    b. To enhance my usefulness to others.
    c. To develop humility, making it possible to receive God's help.

As I understand Him, God:
5. Is:
    a. Everything.
    b. Knowledge.
    c. Power.
    d. Love.
    e. Presence.

6. Where is God? Do I believe God is deep down within me?

APPENDIX 6

Meditation (sitting)

1. Father, please direct my thinking, especially divorce it from motives of:
    a. Selfishness.
    b. Self-seeking.
    c. Self-pity.
    d. Resentment.
    e. Fear.
    f. Dishonesty.

   Please clear my thinking of wrong motives.

2. Think about the 24 hours ahead (DO-ing).
   What will I do?

3. Consider my plans for the day (BE-ing).
   Who will I be?

4. Clarify my vision of Your will for me today (intent).
   How can I best serve You?
   What is my vision of Your will for me today?

5. If I feel indecision, pray: Father, please give me an inspiration, an intuitive thought, or a decision. Help me relax and take it easy ... to stop struggling.

Reading

Select some inspirational/informational reading (*Big Book*, Scripture, *Twenty-Four Hours a Day*, *Daily Reflections*, etc.).

Reflection

Be present to the presence of God; allow the Spirit to guide your thoughts, to speak to your heart and soul. Listen deeply!

Conclusion (on my knees)

Please God …

1.	Show me all through the day what my next step is to be.	Knowledge
2.	Give me whatever I need to take care of tasks and problems.	Power
3.	Especially free me from self-will.	Freedom
4.	Show me the way of patience, tolerance, kindliness, and Love.	Love
5.	Allow today's work to provide an opportunity for me to be useful and helpful. What can I do today for the person who is still sick?	Service

Seventh Step Prayer: Pray it.

"My Creator, I am now willing that you should have all of me, good and bad. I pray that you now remove from me every single defect of character which stands in the way of my usefulness to you and my fellows. Grant me strength, as I go out from here, to do your bidding. Amen" (B.B. page 76).

Appendix 7

My Personal Evening Prayer and Meditation Practice

Set Aside Prayer (on my knees)

God, please let me set aside everything that I think I know about myself, my disease (brokenness), the Twelve Steps and You, God, for an open mind and a new experience with myself, my disease (brokenness), the Twelve Steps and especially You, God!

Purpose: Identify and remove obstacles to the sunlight of the Spirit (sitting)

1. *Constructively* review my day (without fear or favor)
    a. Was I: What motives were underneath my:
        - Resentful?
        - Selfish?
        - Dishonest?
        - Afraid?
        - Intentions?
        - Thoughts?
        - Acts?
        - Efforts?
    b. Do I owe an apology?
    c. Have I kept something to myself that should be discussed with another person at once?
    d. Was I kind and loving toward all?
    e. What could I have done better?
    f. Was I thinking of myself most of the time?
    g. Or was I thinking of what I could do for others, of what I could pack into the stream of life?

2. Ask God's forgiveness.

3. Ask what corrective measures should be taken.

4. Thank Him for blessings received.

5. Be willing to try again tomorrow!

6. Conclude with the prayer of St. Francis (on my knees):
"Lord, make me a channel of thy peace;
That where there is hatred, I may bring love;
That where there is wrong, I may bring the spirit of forgiveness;
That where there is discord, I may bring harmony;
That where there is error, I may bring truth;
That where there is doubt, I may bring faith;
That where there is despair, I may bring hope;
That where there are shadows, I may bring light;
That where there is sadness, I may bring joy.
Lord, grant that I may seek rather to comfort than to be comforted;
To understand, than to be understood;
To love, than to be loved.
For it is by self-forgetting that one finds;
It is by forgiving that one is forgiven;
It is by dying that one awakens to eternal life.
Amen."

Appendix 8
Principles

1. Honesty — Fairness and straightforwardness of conduct, adherence to facts; means uprightness of character or action. Honesty implies a refusal to lie, steal, or deceive in any way. — **ACTION** Live in Truth

2. Faith/Hope — Belief and complete confidence in God without logical proof or material evidence. To desire with expectation of fulfillment, to long for with expectation of obtainment, to expect with desire. — **ACTION** Decide to Believe, to Expect

3. Surrender — To yield to the power, control, or possession of another upon compulsion or demand; to give up completely or agree to forego—especially in favor of another; to give oneself up into the power of another; to give oneself over to something (as an influence or course of action). — **ACTION** Decide to Trust

4. Courage — Mental or moral strength to venture, persevere, and withstand danger, fear, or difficulty; courage implies firmness of mind and will in the face of danger or extreme difficulty. — **ACTION** Write / Name the Truth

5. Integrity	An unimpaired condition; soundness; adherence to a code of moral, artistic, or other values; the quality or state of being complete or undivided.	**ACTION** Confess
6. Willingness	Inclined or favorably disposed in mind; ready; prompt to act or respond; done, borne, or accepted of choice or without reluctance; relating to the will or power of choosing.	**ACTION** Name My Defects
7. Humility	Quality or state of being humble; not proud or haughty; not arrogant or assertive; reflecting, expressing, or offered in the spirit of deference or submission.	**ACTION** Accept
8. Brotherly Love	Affection based on benevolence, warm attachment, enthusiasm, or devotion; unselfish concern that freely accepts another in loyalty and seeks their good; the parental concern of God for God's children.	**ACTION** Care
9. Justice	Maintenance or administration of that which conforms to law, especially spiritual; honorable and fair dealing of persons with each other.	**ACTION** Make Reparation; Amend Behavior

APPENDIX 8

10. Discipline	To train or develop by instruction and exercise—especially in self-control; training that corrects, molds, or perfects the mental faculties or moral character; orderly or prescribed conduct or pattern of behavior.	**ACTION** Pay Attention; Be Aware
11. Awareness	Having or showing realization, perception, or knowledge; implies vigilance in observing or alertness in drawing inferences from what one sees or hears.	**ACTION** Pray: Improve Conscious Contact
12. Service	Contribution to the welfare of others.	**ACTION** Love

Appendix 9
Meeting Formats

Big Book Step Study Meeting (A.A.) ....page 119

Big Book Text Study Meeting (A.A.) ....page 122

Big Book Step Workshop (Open) ....page 123

Big Book Step Study Meeting (Open).............................page 126

APPENDIX 9

Big Book Step Study Meeting
(A.A.)

Format
(Assumes meeting is 6:30 to 8:00 P.M.)

Please stand and join me in the Serenity Prayer.

This is a closed meeting of Alcoholics Anonymous.

Read Preamble:
> A.A. is a fellowship of men and women who share their experience, strength, and hope with each other that they may solve their common problem and help others to recover from alcoholism. The only requirement for membership is a desire to stop drinking. There are no dues or fees for A.A. membership; we are self-supporting through our own contributions. A.A. is not allied with any sect, denomination, political party, organization, or institution; does not wish to engage in any controversy; neither endorses nor opposes any causes. Our primary purpose is to stay sober and help other alcoholics to achieve sobriety.

Anyone in their first 30 days of sobriety? Anyone at this meeting for their first time?

Read Group Conscience.
- Our group is committed to the Twelve Steps of A.A. as outlined in the Alcoholics Anonymous *Big Book*.
- Our group is committed to the long form of the Twelve Traditions as outlined in the *Big Book*.
- Our group is committed to the principle of attraction rather than promotion.
- What you hear here and who you see here, stays here.
- This is a cross-talk meeting and sharing may be interrupted if the person sharing is not talking about the step being discussed,

or the step they are now working. If subject being discussed needs further explanation, a member of the group may interrupt for further clarification.

Ask the participants to introduce themselves.

Ask someone to read a portion of Chapter 5, "How It Works" (B.B. page 58).

The discussion tonight is on Step _____. Please limit your discussion to your experience with this step. We are interested only in your experience, not opinions. If you have not worked this step, then discuss the step you are now working. If you have not worked any of the steps, we invite you to listen.

Our Leader for tonight is _____. Our meeting format asks that the speaker read the appropriate step and corresponding long form of the Traditions. The speaker will read pertinent material from the *Big Book* and then share experience on this step—finishing by 7:00 P.M. or sooner. Speaker selects where round-robin sharing begins. To adhere to the principles of humility, we do not applaud the speaker but we extend our thanks.

Turn the meeting over to the speaker.

At 7:30 P.M., pass basket for Seventh Tradition, and continue sharing.

Close meeting promptly at 8:00 P.M. with a prayer.

APPENDIX 9

Traditions of the Meeting

Officer Requirements
- Secretary—Has one or more years sobriety; has completed all Twelve Steps as outlined in the Alcoholics Anonymous *Big Book;* is a regular member of this meeting.
- Treasurer—Has six months or more sobriety; is a regular member of this meeting.

Officers elected in accordance with the principles of the Third Legacy. Everyone has opportunity to state qualified/not qualified, willing/not willing to serve.

This Group's Steering Committee hears all business reports and discusses all issues before deciding if the group needs to be advised. Committee is composed of current and prior secretaries. All Committee Members must have completed the Twelve Steps as outlined in the *Big Book*.

This meeting adheres to the principle of attraction rather than promotion, is listed in all meeting directories, and contributes regularly as suggested by A.A.

Anyone who has completed the Twelve Steps as outlined in the *Big Book* may be a speaker at the meeting. The speakers are asked in advance of the meeting so that they can adequately prepare. Remind speakers before the meeting that the *Big Book* is our only source for reading; no opinions, please.

The Secretary will interrupt anyone who does not stay focused on the step under discussion, or the current step they are working.

This meeting is open to cross-talk at any time.

A new Secretary and Treasurer are elected every six months.

Big Book Text Study Meeting
(A.A.)

Format
(Assumes meeting is 8:00 to 9:30 P.M.)

Preamble: Welcome to the Alcoholics Anonymous *Big Book* Text Study. This is a closed meeting for alcoholics only. All who have a desire to stop drinking are welcome. The purpose of this meeting is to study the *Big Book* and share based upon our experience only.

The Leader/Reader will read a designated portion of the *Big Book*, pausing at times to allow for questions or relevant cross-talk. We suggest all sharing and cross-talk be in first person ("I") statements. We are here to share our experiences, not our opinions. While sharing is encouraged, it is not mandatory.

Read Chapter 11, "A Vision for You" (B.B. page 151), first two paragraphs.

Are there any newcomers? Any visitors from out of town?

Introductions: Let's go around the room and introduce ourselves.

Ask for and recognize birthdays. Birthday celebrants share.

At approximately 8:45 P.M., read a long form tradition, as the group observes the Seventh Tradition. Short break follows.

At approximately 9:25 P.M. read Chapter 11 "A Vision for You" (B.B. page 164), last three paragraphs.

Closing prayers.

Big Book Step Workshop
(Open)

Format
(Assumes meeting is 7:30 to 9:00 P.M.)

Good evening, my name is _____, and I am an alcoholic. Welcome to our *Big Book* Step Workshop.

Please join me in the set aside prayer:
> God, please let me set aside everything that I think I know about myself, my disease (brokenness), the Twelve Steps and You, God, for an open mind and a new experience with myself, my disease (brokenness), the Twelve Steps and especially You, God!

Let's go around the room and introduce ourselves.

This is the foreword as it appeared in the first printing of the *Big Book*. First Edition in 1939:

> "We of Alcoholics Anonymous are more than one hundred men and women who have recovered from a seemingly hopeless state of mind and body. To show other alcoholics precisely how we have recovered is the main purpose of this book. For them, we hope these pages will prove so convincing that no further authentication will be necessary. We think this account of our experiences will help everyone to better understand the alcoholic. Many do not comprehend that the alcoholic is a very sick person. And besides, we are sure that our way of living has its advantages for all."

It is the purpose of this workshop to experience the recovery process as outlined in the *Big Book* so we may better understand and carry out our primary purpose.

Please join me in five minutes of meditation on why we are here: our own personal recovery and to better prepare ourselves to carry the message of recovery to those who still suffer.

(After meditation): Please join me in the Serenity prayer.

We are here to talk about recovery only, and to go through the Twelve Steps as outlined in the *Big Book*. This is not an emotional or intellectual exercise. This is a spiritual exercise so we can experience the recovery process as we go through it together. Cross-talk is allowed in a loving and supportive manner. Please try to relate only your experience with your questions or comments, not your opinions.

Review of written assignments.

Begin review of reading assignment.

Meeting continues for a total of 1 hour and 30 minutes (no break).

New assignments.

Close meeting:
>You are going to meet these new friends in your own community. Near you, others are dying helplessly like people in a sinking ship. If you live in a large place, there are hundreds. High and low, rich and poor, these are future members of our respective twelve-step fellowships. Among them you will make lifelong friends. You will be bound to them with new and wonderful ties, for you will escape disaster together and you will commence shoulder to shoulder your common journey. Then you will know what it

means to give of yourself that others may survive and rediscover life. You will learn the full meaning of "Love thy neighbor as thyself." Thus we grow, and so can you, though you be but one person with this book in your hand. We believe and hope it contains all you will need to begin.

After a moment of silence, conclude with the prayer for transformation:

"Lord, make me a channel of thy peace;
That where there is hatred, I may bring love;
That where there is wrong, I may bring the spirit of forgiveness;
That where there is discord, I may bring harmony;
That where there is error, I may bring truth;
That where there is doubt, I may bring faith;
That where there is despair, I may bring hope;
That where there are shadows, I may bring light;
That where there is sadness, I may bring joy.
Lord, grant that I may seek rather to comfort than to be comforted;
To understand, than to be understood;
To love, than to be loved.
For it is by self-forgetting that one finds;
It is by forgiving that one is forgiven;
It is by dying that one awakens to eternal life.
Amen."

Big Book Step Study Meeting
(Open)

(Assumes meeting is 7:30 to 9:00 P.M.)

Good evening. My name is _____. Welcome to our *Big Book* Step Study meeting.

Please join me in the set aside prayer.

This is a step study meeting, open to everyone. It is based on the statement contained in the Foreword to the First Edition of the Alcoholics Anonymous *Big Book* "…we are sure that our way of living has its advantages for all." This is not a meeting of A.A., Alanon, or any other twelve-step fellowship. This is an all-inclusive meeting dedicated to the Twelve Steps as contained in the *Big Book* We are open to and support all twelve-step fellowships. All of us will need to adapt the First Step to our own particular brokenness.

Please join me in two minutes of meditation on our primary purpose: to have and maintain a personal spiritual awakening and to help others achieve a spiritual awakening through working the Twelve Steps.

After two minutes of silence: Please join me in the Serenity Prayer.

We are a fellowship of men and women who share their experience, strength, and hope with each other in search of a spiritual awakening. There are no dues or fees for participation; we are self-supporting through our own contributions. We are not allied with any sect, denomination, politics, organization, or institution; we do not wish to engage in any controversy; neither do we endorse nor oppose any causes.

Is anyone at this meeting for the first time? Please introduce yourself.

APPENDIX 9

This is a focused meeting and sharing may be interrupted if the person sharing is not talking about the step being discussed, or the step they are now working. If the subject being discussed needs further explanation a member of the group may interrupt for further clarification. You are qualified to ask questions only if you have already completed the step or are currently working on the step we are talking about tonight.

Let's introduce ourselves and identify our specific brokenness.

I have asked _____ to read a portion of Chapter 5 "How it Works."

The discussion tonight is on Step _____. Our speaker for tonight is _____. Our meeting format asks the speaker to read the specific step. The speaker will read pertinent materials from the *Big Book* only and then share their experience on this step, finishing by 8:00 P.M. or sooner.

In order to adhere to the principles of humility, we do not applaud the speaker but we do extend our thanks.

_____ *(speaker's name)*, please share your experience on Step _____.

When the speaker is finished sharing, read the following statement:

Please limit your discussion to your experience with this step. We are interested only in your experience, not opinions. If you have not worked this step, then discuss the step you are now working. If you have not worked any of the steps, we invite you to listen.

The entire purpose of this meeting is to foster a personal spiritual awakening through a thorough application of the Twelve Steps from the *Big Book*. The only purpose for questions is to facilitate this goal.

Therefore, any question that is not motivated by the spirit of helping one another is not appropriate for the meeting and should be restrained. Our format is designed to facilitate and ensure the meeting's focus and motivate, guide, and generally help others to clearly and seriously complete their work of the Twelve Steps. There is no other reason for questions or comments.

We pass the basket to ensure we are self-supporting *(circulate basket)*.

Would those who came in after the introductions please introduce themselves.

Remember, please limit your sharing to three minutes.

Start the sharing; ask—"Is there anyone who was at the last meeting who didn't get a chance to share?"

_____ *(speaker's name),* please choose where you would like to start the sharing.

Close meeting when everyone has shared or no later than 8:55 P.M. with the reading of "A Vision for You" (B.B. page 164.)

> "Our book is meant to be suggestive only. We realize we know only a little. God will constantly disclose more to you and to us. Ask God in your morning meditation what you can do each day for the person who is still sick. The answers will come, if your own house is in order. But obviously you cannot transmit something you haven't got. See to it that your relationship with God is right, and great events will come to pass for you and countless others. This is the Great Fact for us.
>
> Abandon yourself to God as you understand God. Admit your faults to God and to your fellows. Clear away the wreckage of your past. Give freely of what you find and join us. We shall be with you in the

APPENDIX 9

Fellowship of the Spirit and you will surely meet some of us as you trudge the Road of Happy Destiny.

May God bless you and keep you—until then."

Please join me in the St. Francis prayer:
"Lord, make me a channel of thy peace;
That where there is hatred, I may bring love;
That where there is wrong, I may bring the spirit of forgiveness;
That where there is discord, I may bring harmony;
That where there is error, I may bring truth;
That where there is doubt, I may bring faith;
That where there is despair, I may bring hope;
That where there are shadows, I may bring light;
That where there is sadness, I may bring joy.
Lord, grant that I may seek rather to comfort than to be comforted;
To understand, than to be understood;
To love, than to be loved.
For it is by self-forgetting that one finds;
It is by forgiving that one is forgiven;
It is by dying that one awakens to eternal life.
Amen."

Please stand and join me in the Lord's Prayer.

Notes

Notes

Notes

Notes

Notes